T0339480

"There's no one more qualified to teach operational resilience than Mike Janko. Mike's leadership of Goodyear's business continuity efforts have seen us through issues of all kinds, and he is an expert we trust to ensure we maintain service to our customers during unexpected challenges. I encourage leaders in all industries to read *Excellence in Operational Resilience* to learn from the journey Mike and our teams follow in supporting our employees and our business operations. Readers will connect with the way Mike faces difficulties head on, with optimism, an empowering managerial style and of course, resilience."

Gary S. VanderLind, SHRM-SCP, *senior vice president and chief human resources officer at The Goodyear Tire & Rubber Company*

"Over the past twenty years I've had the chance to work with Mike and his teams to plan for and respond to dozens of hurricanes, winter storms and supply chain challenges. Our support of associates, the communities where we operate, and business operations were top priorities. Following each situation, we assessed our process to close any gaps and improve upon our future efforts. Through these coordinated efforts, we recovered quickly from every challenge and thrived as a team. *Excellence in Operational Resilience* shares successful strategies proven over multiple decades. Mike's method of leading, following and guiding the way enables every team member to contribute, provide their expertise and remain aligned on a common path, ultimately leading to outstanding performance. We take pride in knowing that regardless of the crisis we may face, the support for our associates, the communities where we operate, and business operations will be executed well, and negative impact will be minimized."

Brad Ioerger, *general manager chemical operations and commercial at The Goodyear Tire & Rubber Company*

"I wholeheartedly endorse *Excellence in Operational Resilience* by Mike Janko! This book is a testament to his remarkable leadership in the challenging field of Business Continuity. I have personally worked with Mike managing hurricanes, tornadoes, and various crises, Mike's expertise in operational resilience shines through. The practical strategies shared, from documenting a roadmap to risk management and team alignment, are invaluable for any organization. The focus on turning risks into opportunities is a game-changer for achieving sustainable business results and financial stability. Witnessing the impact of the material and processes featured by Mike in real life, I highly recommend this book to all seeking business resilience in the face of adversity."

Billy Ray Taylor, *retired Goodyear operations executive and CEO of LinkedXL*

"*Excellence in Operational Resilience* is a must read for both seasoned resilience professionals and relative newcomers alike! Mike has a proven ability to effectively lead and manage global teams through extremely challenging and novel risks affecting people, communities, and business operations. *Excellence in Operational Resilience* combines teaching both the basic technical skills along with strategic decision analysis that helps the reader think like an executive. The tie between personal and operational resilience reminds you that the journey will not always be easy, yet the results can lead to competitive advantages."

Jerome Ryan, *chief risk and compliance officer at Carbonaires*

"When introducing a culture of health into an organization, emergency preparedness is a key component aligning operational resilience into business continuity planning. Mike Janko served as a valued partner and leader over a decade working together. We successfully navigated through dozens of global events and crises, including the complexities of the COVID-19 pandemic. Mike's ability to adequately assess a local situation and its impact for the enterprise permitted him to lead individuals and managers within the organization through the immediate and longer-term tactical needs to recovery. Along with continuous process improvement, his leadership established a true roadmap for operational resilience."

J. Brent Pawlecki, MD, *chief health officer*

"I've been witness to Mike embodying the characteristics of a resilient leader for decades. Regardless of his rank in the martial arts, world sit up records and other accomplishments, he remains strongly connected to and supportive of "everyone on the team". His philosophy of leading, following and guiding the way applies the right perspective and focuses on positive outcomes rather than being a victim of circumstance. Mike's references to turning risks into opportunities, aligning teams, exceeding objectives and continuous improvement carries over into his personal and professional activities. Excellence in both operational and personal resilience blend together well in the examples shared throughout his book."

Steve A. Kovacs, *author and Soke of Minna Jiu-Jitsu*

"*Excellence in Operational Resilience* provides a valuable roadmap with hands-on examples of how to set goals, exceed them and incorporate lessons learned throughout your organization. Mike's method of applying soft skills, behaviors and technical knowledge can bring immediate success in an easy to understand and apply manner. Mike has personally led response to over 3,000 significant business events on every continent. His ability to lead, follow and guide is embedded in his DNA and is evident in everything he does. I've known Mike for over 4 decades, and when he sets a goal to do something you can count on it!"

Jim Folger, *president of OneSource Technical, Inc.*

"Mike Janko's engaging approach in building *Excellence in Operational Resilience* is a model for not only the manufacturing industry. Colleges and Universities have proven that collaborative efforts with external agencies are critical components of resilient organizations. Mike's work with AICUO led to sharing of best practices and strategies that benefitted our member institutions. Align the right teams, deploy the right strategies, and have the right objectives to create a resilience awareness culture."

C. Todd Jones, *president and general counsel at Association of Independent Colleges & Universities of Ohio*

Excellence in Operational Resilience

Providing essential guidance to thrive in a complex environment, this book showcases tools to take the leadership role in the process of building resilience in any organization in a timely, effective, and practical way for today's risks and tomorrow's challenges.

All organizations seek to be resilient, yet most do not have a clear definition of what that means for them, or a plan to manage the journey to attain it. This resilience playbook includes the right combination of technical knowledge, team structure, leadership support, and behavioral competencies, all based on a clear "Lead, Follow, Guide" framework. Based on the author's three decades of successfully implementing resilience-based strategies at Goodyear and other major firms, this book offers road-tested advice and techniques to bring quick wins and long-term success in organizational resilience.

With this book to assist, risk-savvy executive leaders and professionals working in business continuity, risk management, security, IT, supply chain, operations management, and process improvement will maintain a constant pulse on their journey towards resilience, keep the right people engaged, and create a team-based approach to reach their goals.

Michael W. Janko is Goodyear's Director of Global Business Continuity, and the company's global enterprise leader in development and application of resilience-based policies, procedures, protocols, and guidance to provide immediate positive strategic business impact. He holds multiple certifications in business continuity and risk management, including Master Business Continuity Professional (MBCP), Master Business Continuity Institute (MBCI), Certified Business Continuity Lead Auditor (CBCLA), and Associate in Risk Management (ARM). He effectively managed response and recovery to over 3,000 business continuity events, crises, or incidents (including for Stouffer Hotels, Nestle, and Goodyear) over 30 years. Michael has also taught courses, classes, and workshops at Cleveland State University and Cuyahoga Community College, and led training for AICUO, which represents all the independent colleges and universities in Ohio.

Excellence in Operational Resilience

How to Lead, Follow and Guide the Way

Michael W. Janko

Routledge
Taylor & Francis Group

NEW YORK AND LONDON

Designed cover image: NiseriN and edb3_16 / © Getty Images

First published 2024
by Routledge
605 Third Avenue, New York, NY 10158

and by Routledge
4 Park Square, Milton Park, Abingdon, Oxon, OX14 4RN

Routledge is an imprint of the Taylor & Francis Group, an informa business

Library of Congress Cataloging-in-Publication Data
Names: Janko, Michael W., author.
Title: Excellence in operational resilience: how to lead, follow and guide the way / Michael W. Janko.
Description: New York, NY: Routledge, 2024. | Includes bibliographical references and index. | Identifiers: LCCN 2023044811 (print) | LCCN 2023044812 (ebook) | ISBN 9781032572857 (hardback) | ISBN 9781032572840 (paperback) | ISBN 9781003438700 (ebook)
Subjects: LCSH: Organizational resilience. | Resilience (Personality trait) | Organizational sociology. | Leadership.
Classification: LCC HD58.9.J25 2024 (print) | LCC HD58.9 (ebook) | DDC 658.4/06--dc23/eng/20231005
LC record available at https://lccn.loc.gov/2023044811
LC ebook record available at https://lccn.loc.gov/2023044812

ISBN: 978-1-032-57285-7 (hbk)
ISBN: 978-1-032-57284-0 (pbk)
ISBN: 978-1-003-43870-0 (ebk)

DOI: 10.4324/9781003438700

Typeset in Sabon
by SPi Technologies India Pvt Ltd (Straive)

"The only thing harder than being resilient is explaining why you aren't!"
To the many individuals and teams who joined my journey to lead, follow, and guide the way toward personal and operational resilience.

Contents

Acknowledgements

My sincerest love for my mom and dad who were the best role models one could have. They came to this country as immigrants and taught me their Hungarian and Transylvanian work ethic and heritage. Their love, prayers, compassion, and sacrifices showed me how faith and family keep you well grounded.

I extend my heartfelt thanks to my wife Debbie and our family—Brad, Brittany, Vlora, Brian, and Ian—for their love and support throughout my career and the writing of this book. I cannot say enough about what you mean to me. Thanks, Debbie, for being my top supporter in our decades-long journey through life and work.

I am extremely grateful for having the opportunity to work with thousands of Goodyear associates at all levels in the Americas, EMEA, Asia Pacific, and Global Technology. You all had critical roles on our governance committee, as regional leaders, and with tactical support in responding to thousands of extremely challenging crises and events. While other organizations struggled to address a crisis, we moved forward and followed our roadmap. You helped convince our associates and our business contacts we had their best interests in focus, we were responding effectively, and we would do our best to gain knowledge from our response and remain resilient. You are all part of leading, following, and guiding the way.

It's been a great privilege and honor to serve on the board of directors of DRI International for over a decade. Using the Professional Practices to develop and maintain operational resilience since 9/11 has proven to be a solid basis for remaining resilient.

I am grateful for the lessons I learned from my 40+ year journey with The Mayfield Academy of Jiu Jitsu and Karate. Joining the dojo led me to realize the importance of overcoming physical and mental challenges that I apply to overcoming operational risks and challenges.

Special thanks to my Routledge publishing team. The advice, guidance, and feedback I received from Senior Editor Business and Management

Meredith Norwich, Editorial Assistants Rupert Spurrier and Bethany Nelson, and Production Editor Eleonora Kouneni helped me to deliver my message in the way intended.

Finally, thanks to everyone who supported me in the research, development, and implementation of strategies shared in this book. You reinforced that this is the most effective approach toward leading, following, and guiding the way toward excellence in operational resilience.

Preface

Here are the standards for your operations to be resilient... Other books on resilience may start that way, but my book does not. Striving for excellence in operational resilience is a journey with a roadmap. Combining technical skills with the right personal behaviors and attributes of a resilient leader is the method I used for achieving operational resilience.

I've had the pleasure of successfully managing extremely challenging events throughout my career with thousands of people from dozens of countries, languages, and cultures. We remained focused on associates first and business operations next, and recognized teammates for their outstanding work. Their positive behaviors played a big role in our success. The best feedback you can receive is when a major crisis is resolved and the responding team and their leadership tell you, "We appreciated your leadership and help because you did not judge us—you helped us."

In the years since I worked at Nestle, came to Goodyear, and started our business continuity process, all of our associates and leadership thrived with this approach. We had support at every level, were allowed to take liberties, did cutting edge work, and asked for forgiveness later. Egos took a back seat to our focus on reaching team goals. I've observed and benchmarked other resilient leaders and their teams on every level and sector if it appeared that they were doing better than us. What I found was most high performing and successful teams have continuous improvement in their DNA, allowing them to take the most effective actions and make the most effective choices.

I obtained my extreme competitiveness by learning from my close circle of friends and those I admired in the martial arts and in competitive sports. As part of my personal continuous improvement, I view risks as challenges I cannot lose. To be world class or best in class requires an extreme time commitment; a strong work ethic; the ability to withstand stress, pain, and pressure; the effective management of conflicting workloads; being blessed; and a little bit of luck. They are key components of being resilient.

Along the way, I also observed how behaviors were critical to success in meeting objectives and goals to be world class and best in class. I realized *my* ideas needed to become *our* ideas, while I provided guidance and vision along the way. To this day, I take pride in seeing others I've worked with move on to other roles, carry the same mindset, and share this philosophy with their teams.

I realized the need to apply the same strategy used in conditioning an athlete to conditioning teams:

- Leveraging repetition, blocking out time, learning from what you and others do well, and being able to bounce back when you don't execute well.
- Having the knowledge, following your roadmap, influencing with the right behaviors, and continuously improving yourself and your operations.
- Attaining and maintaining resilience.
- Having the ability to lead, follow, and guide the way.

That is how this book and the advice I am sharing came about. Whether you consider yourself new to seeking resilience or best in class at doing so, you'll find the approach in my book unique and one to benchmark.

Chapter 1

Introduction

You can tell when an organization is truly resilient or when it continues to struggle to effectively address an unexpected obstacle it has faced. Its immediate actions and responses are displayed though public and social media. The longer-term impact is evident from the reactions of customers, shareholders, associates (employees), and the public. According to the Federal Emergency Management Agency (FEMA)[1], 40 percent of businesses do not reopen following a disaster. In addition, another 25 percent fail to reopen within the following year. The United States Small Business Association[2] reported that over 90 percent of companies struck by a disaster fail within two years. Organizations have varying terms for a "disaster". A disaster can be considered a sudden, unplanned catastrophic event causing unacceptable damage or loss, and is interchangeably referred to by some as an emergency, crisis, incident, or bad thing.

Over the years, popular terms have been used to describe overcoming obstacles. When it comes to people, we recognise someone who is "resilient" if they are strong, persistent, tenacious, and tough. We recognise an organization as being "resilient" when it thrives regardless of the challenges it faces. Resilient organizations rebound, continuously improve, and have a competitive advantage.

The following chapters provide guidance on overcoming obstacles from an operational perspective. By structuring, developing, maintaining, and improving an overall strategy for operating under adverse conditions, your operations and organization are well on their way to being resilient. Included are lessons learned from my perspective as a leader, teacher, and administrator of programs that are integral to this journey. I will reference tools used, strategies implemented, and takeaways on the importance of what you do, along with examples of beneficial competency behaviors. This may be viewed as a new approach as it does not strictly reference compliance standards and definitions. You do not need to be 100 percent accurate in execution all the time. Instead, a greater emphasis is placed on building upon the strengths in your organization. In leading the process,

DOI: 10.4324/9781003438700-1

follow feedback from the right team members, and then guide the organization along the way toward operational resilience.

Individuals and their teams are truly resilient when they have an ability to be their most effective, regardless of challenges. Resilient teams face difficulties head on. They maintain control of situations, have no shortage of new ways to tackle issues, and emerge stronger after addressing challenges. By structuring the right teams, using the right tools, and implementing the right behaviors, you better the odds of a positive outcome to help promote organizational resilience.

Why it's Important

"Resilience" is defined as having the ability to embrace, adapt, maintain, and improve. To be ready for and recover rapidly from setbacks and disruptions. To be "tough". It is defined in many ways including the overall management of risk. By having an expansive view of resilience, risks are better managed, critical processes are well maintained, and you thrive regardless of expected and unforeseen circumstances. All organizations benefit by having a process in place to manage risk effectively. The ones doing that the best have resilient leaders who know how to balance a variety of challenges. Business continuity, risk management, crisis management, and service continuity (IT disaster recovery) programs and disciplines all help support that effort. Leadership at all levels conduct risk-based decision making, although they may have a slightly different take on risks based on their responsibilities, training, and networking. Although a Board Chair, Chief Financial Officer, Chief Risk Officer, Chief Operating Officer, and all other "Chief" level leaders have different teams they lead, they do share a common interest—they seek to have resilient teams and conduct resilient operations. This promotes a resilient organization. By having keen insight into the perspective of chief level leaders, you can communicate common resilience goals more easily.

Operational resilience integrates all operational activities under one clear management structure. It is an expansion of business continuity management programs to focus on the risk appetite, tolerance levels, and impacts to both internal and external stakeholders. A clear commitment from management and the board is key to the right view of risks, strategies, and benefits. Measuring the long-term value of organizational resilience benefits the business over traditional metrics that showcase short-term cost savings. A short-term commitment is often made to operational resilience, and that short-term commitment will fade once the current crisis is resolved. Strategic advantage can be gained by having a more expansive view. Maintaining focus will help to absorb stress and enable the organization to thrive by capitalizing on opportunities when your competitors cannot.

The overall commitment to operational resilience is a driver of value to your organization.

The importance of personal resilience in the right operational leader roles cannot be overlooked. Let's agree on our definition of personal resilience and on a few of the characteristics needed to be resilient as a leader when managing challenging activities, events, and crises.

Being personally resilient means:

- Having the mental strength to face difficulties head on.
- Effectively handling stress during crises.
- Understanding that challenges help support the ability to adapt and succeed.

We will continue to reference the following characteristics that a leader needs to be resilient:

- Optimism: Looking for the positive aspects of every event and focusing on what will be gained in the long term.
- Perspective: Avoiding overreactions and not exaggerating what you are dealing with.
- Accepting change: Focusing on what you can control and knowing that change is part of life's journey.
- Adjustable: Modifying your schedule to help address challenging situations.
- Sense of humor: Maintaining the ability to see the lighter side of any event to help you stay optimistic and allowing this to carry over to others.
- In shape: Being physically ready to take on challenges by quieting your mind and focusing on keeping your body physically fit.
- Gratitude: Remembering the positives to help you stay focused and lead through challenges.
- Survivor: Viewing yourself as the one who will lead a positive outcome rather than being a victim of circumstance.
- In control: Taking the right actions and addressing the right work-streams instead of waiting for others to resolve the problem.
- Self-compassion: Knowing when it is necessary to take a break promotes your overall health and prepares you to face the next challenge.
- Hopeful: Anticipating change and helping to drive it while knowing you cannot change the past.

The requirements for avoiding and managing risk, along with other compliance-related activities and standards, are also just good business practice. Some may differ by your type of business, and others are common to all. Manufacturing, retail, finance, government, education, utilities, and all other business sectors continually make risk-based decisions. Investors, regulators, and customers expect success in the overall management of risk. Resilient organizations will experience positive quarterly earnings directly reflecting the stability of an organization.

Associates (employees) and their families rely on companies to execute resilience activities effectively. Their ability to not only earn a paycheck but to grow in their roles, support the company's goals, and take pride in their work reflects resilience. In addition, the media's ability to report in real time on your effective management of business challenges plays a key role in keeping focus on what a successfully resilient organization does.

The goal should be to remain focused on resilience with a well-developed and consistently implemented process. Once your journey is underway, you realize every obstacle is an opportunity and every challenge will lead to a lesson learned.

Why Some Fail and Some Succeed

"Just because someone makes it look easy, doesn't mean it is." This statement applies to many organizational topics including this one. Advice is readily available on how to become resilient, yet applying this theory in practice is a challenge. Having part of the solution is being partially successful. I've seen numerous instances where an organization begins their journey toward resilience by naming someone as their leader because that person has been recognized as being successful in part of the overall resilience process. They build on their knowledge and can be well on their road to resilience if they and their teams have the right skills and the right competencies. Others implement what they have a comfort level in executing yet lose sight of the bigger picture. There are times when using what you have in place works, other times it doesn't. A few reasons why a named leader may not be quite staged for success include:

- A lack of understanding of the components of the entire resilience process. Looking at the bigger picture gives you a better insight into what's needed to succeed.
- Not staying the course on a long-term plan. You will likely face setbacks, although consistency in attaining objectives, goals, and targets is critical to success.
- An inability to adapt actions and plans to your corporate culture. You might have great vision and meticulous focus, but knowing how to best implement the right steps, at the right time, and the right way is necessary.

- Relying on an individual or company who does not have a complete understanding of your organization's practices, habits, and people. You need the right blend of external support and internal knowledge to be most effective.
- Using negative versus positive feedback methods during challenges. Your team remembers not only what you accomplished. How you did it is equally important.
- A lack of balance between targeted results and team behaviors. The goal is to stay a strong team that wants to stay engaged and that enjoys working together.
- Lack of knowledge in how to effectively manage the scope of the goal. Make sure your team continues to have the right people in the right roles.
- Having non-resilient based leadership in critical roles. The tactical functions that are part of the team are all equally important as those of the team's leader.
- An inability to lead, follow, and guide the way. This process will be explained shortly.

Those who succeed in their resilience journey have the right combination of technical expertise and personal skills to put theories into practice, deal with human element issues, and use effective core competency behaviors to keep moving forward and continually improve. They know how to be effective at:

- Finding something they are "really good at".
- Staying focused on being an "influence manager" to sell important concepts.
- Being curious and always learning with a "continuous improvement mindset"; and
- Working to "know their topic better than anyone else in the room."

Resilient leaders know that what they are undertaking may be incredibly difficult to manage. They possess a belief that is unshakable, they hate to lose, and they can guide others through uncertainty. They effectively engage and lead others in a common purpose while maintaining a positive outlook—not just at a single level, but at every level including leadership and in tactical and functional roles.

Operationally resilient organizations build resilience into business groups and functions. Their investments in resilience are a long-term commitment instead of quick savings for short-term benefits. They utilize adaptive business metrics to avoid short-term gains and results. They view their advantage over competitors as a critical metric, including quicker recovery rates, minimized business interruption and negative cost impacts. Their use of business continuity and risk management tools to anticipate future crises and events, plan for their occurrence and identify key actions are part of the resilience process. Crises are viewed as competitive opportunities to plan for instead of "once in a great while" disruptions. Investments are made in resilience supportive tools and activities. Having resilience champions at the right level of the organization changes the culture from being reactive to proactive. These champions have a view of the long term, versus the short term and stand up for their beliefs during the worst economic times. Continuous improvement actions based on lessons learned may have short-term negative cost impacts but many long-term benefits.

What's Your Best Option?

You may have heard the quote: "Lead, Follow or Get Out of the Way". This statement has been attributed to both military leaders Thomas Paine[3] and General George S. Patton[4]. Their application of the term was during The American Revolution and during World War II, where extreme challenges required extreme alignment of teams. Paine's and Patton's leadership philosophies were necessary and applicable. Most of us were not around when this mindset proved to be successful. Times have changed. The focus on team leadership, influence management, and adaptability has evolved.

The philosophy to "lead, follow and guide the way" is critical to operational resilience and to becoming a resilient organization. Having a blend of knowing what to do, gaining team feedback, and staying aligned to your forward plan to be resilient benefits a wide-ranging audience. It's a philosophy I've implemented successfully through some very challenging crises. Benchmarking indicates some others have not done so well. Having the right team-building philosophy is critical to successful team engagement. You want to succeed yet not leave a trail of destruction when done, since you and your organization will then not be as effective or as resilient going forward. You want to build on your success most effectively and the right philosophy and behaviors will help you get there.

Core Competency Focus

Certain core competency behaviors will make you a better leader and will enable you to follow better and guide the way more effectively. They are referenced as you progress through concepts in this book. The importance of core competency behaviors and the specific ones highlighted in the journey toward resilience cannot be overlooked. They are the personality characteristics and behaviors needed to be successful in attaining the resilience goals outlined in this text. They include skills, actions, and qualities to be a top resilience performer. They contribute to the ability to assume bigger roles and greater responsibility. They are critical in selecting the right team members to succeed in your resilience journey. Various organizations reference behavioral competencies in their leadership and associate training, ranging from a few to dozens. Five specific ones that we will focus on for success in operational resilience include:

- **Situational awareness:** Knowing where you are, what is going on around you, and selecting the right activities on which to focus. Having a more accurate sense of reality during anarchy, which allows your organization's operations to be more alert and to make better decisions. Assigning team members to the right priorities and being aware of the potential risks in making certain decisions. Failing to maintain situational awareness can compound a crisis or escalate a situation to a crisis when it should not be one. Balancing all the workstreams during a business continuity event is critical since any one of them can escalate to a critical path item in no time. Making smart decisions is reflective of situational awareness.
- **Agility:** Approaching work with curiosity, speed, and purpose; embracing change; and eliminating complexity. Agility includes seeing possibilities during unknown situations and taking quick action to turn these opportunities into results or into new ways of managing the team. Teammates gain confidence when receiving clear and concise advice and coaching. By providing simple instructions in complex situations, teams gain confidence and can make significant progress. It's all about stabilizing the team during chaotic conditions with clear direction. This in turn provides productivity, efficiency, and motivation.
- **Promoting collaboration:** Operating as one team, engaging in open dialogue, and leveraging diverse points of view to help the organization succeed. Credit is distributed skillfully so the team gets the right accolades for shared success and individuals who provided significant contributions are rewarded. Seeking out others' ideas and perspectives in conversations will promote team resilience. Simplifying and improving team response both internally and externally is executed well. Diversity of perspectives when making decisions on behalf of teams is regularly in place.
- **Energizing the team:** Creating an environment that inspires and giving the best in everything you do. Show trust in teammates by empowering them to make key contributions. Each team member is given opportunities to use their unique skills, abilities, passion, and voice. The team becomes highly motivated with a great deal of energy. Taking time to regularly celebrate efforts, progress, and everyday wins so all are inspired to keep moving ahead.

- **Delivering results**: Seizing opportunities and making courageous decisions helps to achieve business goals and capabilities for the future. The team is results focused with everyone engaged in productive behaviors without poor performance. Everyone is pushed through setbacks and obstacles. A great deal of energy and emphasis is placed on excellence, even in the most difficult times. A strong sense of urgency is placed on exceeding goals and beating deadlines. The team consistently delivers results and accelerates both short- and long-term goals.

Benefits for You

You should become truly aligned and resilient across all levels of your operations and organization. Do this with the right competency behaviors so you build and maintain support in your goals. This concept has proven to be of great value in all human, natural, and technological challenges. Below are a few examples of recent events that showcase behaviors for a resilient organizational response. You will see additional details on these and other events throughout the book that highlight effective implementation of resilience-based strategies.

Infectious Disease (ID) responses required extreme agility, effective collaboration, energized teams and results delivery. The situational awareness actions required an immediate comprehensive response by a wide-ranging team. It required resilience. Goodyear had already developed protocols in response to previous ID events like Bird Flu, Swine Flu, and Norovirus. We developed ID protocols to fit our business, conducted tabletop exercises (discussion-based simulations and scenarios) on multiple occasions for ID outbreaks, and had teams identified, trained, and ready to go. When the initial Asia Pacific based pandemic broke out in 2019, we put our plan into action, yet this was one of the most difficult crises to manage due to the extent of its impact and global involvement. It affected every person, business, and community and played out in real time in social media during a US election year. It included involvement across all levels of the company and partnerships with external authorities, suppliers, customers, families, and the community. The need to immediately assess its impact on our associates and the business was immediate, and it was critical that we engaged teams across all levels of our organization. Our previous ID plans were all updated with support from associates throughout all regions. As complexity was abundant, so was the goal to explain and provide guidance for what became known as COVID-19 and additional variants in easily understood terminology. In addition, it became critical for us to find a way to process and explain variations in guidance from health services and the government. The need to develop and implement protocols for shutting down facilities and business operations were complex as were the immediate impacts to global travel, supply chains, and availability of resources. Keeping everyone healthy and engaged while working remotely was expected, and new ways to communicate and convince our audience that we will get through this together were needed.

Well-established organizations and upstart companies alike all struggled with the challenges imposed by COVID-19. Stakeholders needed to be energized, and to be successful, they needed to convey a vision focused on what's best for all—a vision of resilience. Terms like the new normal, hybrid work, limited hours, asymptomatic, hand hygiene, social distancing, and self-isolation were common. For many it lasted three years in team response and recovery and changed the way businesses made decisions on people, benefits, business relationships, work methods, etc.

Geopolitical risks (war, protests, violence) included the Russian invasion of Ukraine and China's escalation in Taiwan. Many had not experienced the potential for, and actual war in decades. They presented challenges as those presented by ID referenced above. In addition, financial sanctions were added to the mix. The US and European Union jointly identified individuals who were financially sanctioned. Citizens and companies were prevented from legally doing business with the financially sanctioned entities.

Goodyear had associates, facilities, raw materials, and finished goods at risk from Russia's invasion. The immediate need was to ensure everyone was safe and accounted for. We then needed to identify alternate sources for raw materials and finished goods as part of retail and manufacturing. This included single and sole source suppliers who were at risk with long delivery lead times. Their recovery from the ID outbreak further complicated their ability to meet their contractual requirements. Once again, operational resilience-based actions included the need for teams to be aware, agile, collaborative, energized and delivering results to succeed.

Ransomware events have reportedly increased over 50 percent annually[5] over the past few years. Their advanced techniques to make financial gains continue to evolve and are a real threat to all organizations. Planning for and responding to these threats requires quick implementation of IT security and cyber planning. Goodyear's teams continue to do outstanding work in managing potential for impacts to our associates and business operations. These teams are key to our operational resilience. Ransomware risks will likely remain for many years to come. Examples of organizations well prepared for ransomware risks may not be obvious to the public. Those that are held to ransom and do not do so well have quarterly or annual earnings impacts shared via the media. They are examples of organizations lacking in resilience success. Many of the process components for being resilient were needed due to reliance on critical partners and suppliers who were affected. Their resilience-based activities or lack of them had a far-reaching effect on others. Among the behaviors that were critical to success included awareness, agility, collaboration, energized teams, and effectively delivering results.

As we consider other recent major events and crises, it becomes evident how well planned and executed actions and behaviors lead to positive results. The need to create an environment where your teams naturally work together and do great things is the new baseline. Are you identifying and preparing for the top ten risks you're presently facing, and can you adapt your approach easily? Are your teams trained for and embracing that concept? Modern vulnerabilities call for innovative processes and tools for embedding resilience and managing risk. How you structure, support, and improve upon your business continuity, crisis management, and risk management process is critical.

Our Journey Toward Excellence in Operational Resilience

Below is an overview of the framework followed throughout the book, so you know what to expect and how the recommendations, examples, and actual experiences tie together. You can reference the chapters to validate what you have in place and reflect upon your own journey and the progress you've made. In addition, they can help you to identify gaps you may have in your process, find solutions that apply, and ultimately enable you to improve upon your resilience journey.

Introduction

Operational and personal resilience both play a key role in overcoming obstacles. The approach you take should include the most effective technical and behavioral competencies which help to promote more effective team engagement and results.

Document Your Roadmap

There are effective management tools you will use in your journey toward resilience. Having a well-defined process and structure will help to define the value of resilience and reinforce its strategic and competitive advantage.

Turning Risk into Opportunity

Risk-based decision making is integral to organizational resilience and works well when you have a well-defined and aligned process across your organization. Identifying and effectively managing all risks, incidents, and crises helps promote a competitive advantage in resilient organizations.

Aligning Your Teams

Form the right teams at both the strategic and tactical levels. Align with the right leaders in your organization who can be your resilience champions as you continue to gain momentum.

Resilient Deployment

Deploying your resilience plan includes implementing the tools you've identified to be best suited to your operations. As you encounter expected and unexpected results, your team's execution of behavioral competencies will help determine the degree of your success.

Objectives Overcome Obstacles

It is unlikely that you will always be satisfied with the resources, funding, and amount of time to do what you think is needed. Have a common objective and metrics that critical team members can target and are committed to completing.

Maturity Model

Define expectations across the organization. Consider developing a maturity model that identifies what "good, better and best" looks like and determine the level your organization is committed to attaining.

Maintaining Momentum

Identify a baseline and set targets for continuous improvement. Gain value from internal and external resources who help continue to lead, follow, and guide the way.

Helping You Lead, Follow and Guide the Way

My operational resilience journey began as a mechanical engineer with Stouffer Hotels where I managed new construction and retrofit of hotels in the United States. My responsibilities included handling significant issues in hotels during fires, hurricanes, human element, and technological events. It continued with risk management activities in hotels, restaurants, manufacturing plants, and logistics centers for Stouffer's parent company Nestle Enterprises following a merger with Nestle USA.

I left Nestle and became Goodyear's Loss Prevention and Control Manager. I had proposed a business continuity process at Goodyear just prior to the onset of 9/11. We had business continuity underway at Nestle USA, and I knew it would be of immediate business value to Goodyear. While there was little interest by management when I first proposed it, I continued to research and repackage materials to develop the scope, structure, and roadmap for a successful business continuity program. My research included benchmarking programs at two companies. One was a major customer of Goodyear. Another was the previous employer of Goodyear's new chairman. The morning of 9/11, I sent a PowerPoint deck directly to the chairman with a brief email describing how 9/11 was the crisis and business continuity event of our lifetime and offered to assist if needed. He contacted me immediately. We met and set Goodyear's business continuity process in motion. Since then, I've managed over 3,000 events and crises with cross-functional teams following the same process I proposed on 9/11.

If your organization sees the value of business continuity and operational resilience without experiencing a once in a lifetime crisis, that's great! If not, you'll need to tap into your own personal resilience. Be persistent and be ready and able to explain in many ways to many people at all levels in your organization why a business continuity program is vital to your organization's success. Keep pushing forward when others push back and learn how to adapt to your organization's culture. It is also important that you find the right champion. Your chairman or another leader in your organization may be your champion like mine was. A little bit of luck helps too!

My multi-decade journey toward operational resilience continues. Many of the examples shared with you come from my background and experience as Goodyear's Director of Global Business Continuity. Every role I've had taught me valuable lessons on motivation, facing risks, and influence management and on how to lead, follow, and guide the way.

The scope of international resilience-based teams I've participated with, and lead involve Goodyear's operations with $20 billion in annual sales that include 49 factories, 76 logistic centers, 600 suppliers, and 70,000 employees. It includes being a global enterprise leader in the development and application of business continuity and operational resilience-based policies, procedures, protocols, and guidance providing immediate positive strategic business impact. Holding multiple certifications in business continuity and risk management helps to make better decisions. Goodyear's Business Continuity process has been recognized both internally and externally as a competitive advantage. Our planning for pandemics was recognized as a best practice in the private sector.

Recent challenges we've met to maintain operational resilience included global crises like ID outbreaks, China Zero Covid Lockdown, Russia's invasion of Ukraine, supplier ransomware, and natural crises (hurricanes, earthquakes, and flooding). Goodyear's teams managed them effectively in supporting associates, business operations, and the community with a focus on operational resilience.

Being the first-generation American son of Hungarian immigrants instilled many life lessons in me that I still follow today. I've shared them with my children and friends as well. My parents emigrated to the United States with few possessions. They had a unique work ethic, believed in the importance of family, faith, and traditions they followed for generations. My experiences and the work ethic instilled in me created a drive to succeed in every activity I undertake. My view is that being focused on a balance of mental and physical challenges makes you thrive and keeps you resilient. Having reached a rank of 5th Degree Black Belt in Minna Jiu Jitsu, setting a world record in Marine Corps style sit ups, and winning numerous corporate cardio fitness challenges are examples of how I've achieved and maintained resilience and have thrived in physical challenges.

My journey engaging teams in leading, following, and guiding toward operational resilience continues in a variety of ways, including empowering others to be the most effective in the management of risks. I am thrilled to be able to share some of what has worked for me and for teams I've led, and I'm confident it can benefit you as well.

Notes

1 https://www.fema.gov/
2 https://www.sba.gov/business-guide/manage-your-business/prepare-emergencies
3 https://www.goodreads.com/quotes/997628-lead-follow-or-get-out-of-the-way
4 https://graciousquotes.com/george-patton/
5 https://us.norton.com/blog/emerging-threats/ransomware-statistics

Chapter II

Document Your Roadmap

Resilience Roadmap and Journey

A journey is defined as "an adventure." A roadmap is defined as "a lengthy or complex program." By approaching resilience as an adventure through a lengthy program, you create a positive outlook for yourself and your teams. Roadmaps are great for looking for short- and long-term priorities. If done well, you can rally everyone effectively toward reaching strategic goals with the best outcomes. Roadmaps can also be practical ways of organizing, highlighting, and focusing on common objectives, goals, and measures. Here are a few suggestions for how to begin and maneuver through your operational resilience roadmap:

- Assess what tools will be of use to you in initially identifying and communicating your resilience journey and goals. Consider what's outlined in this chapter.
- Consider what objectives your organization is committed to and how your resilience process supports them.
- Define a timeline for getting leadership, strategic, and tactical functions involved.
- Focus on details initially to promote a better understanding of the message you're delivering.
- Keep in mind that planning past the first few months will change as your understanding of a crisis or event increases, so you don't need to be precise in the long term.
- Set reasonable intervals for checking on your progress.
- Communicate your roadmap at a regular frequency, continue to adjust along the journey, and remain transparent.

DOI: 10.4324/9781003438700-2

We will focus on three important roadmap components throughout this book:

1. Developing the plan (including tools and teams).
2. Continually improving upon your plan.
3. Focusing on the right leadership behaviors to gain consensus and to stay aligned on your journey.

Recognizing the value of resilience and how it is of strategic and competitive advantage is critical. Your ability in leading, following, and guiding your teams quickly becomes a benefit to your business. As you proceed in this journey with your roadmap, bear in mind these important concepts:

- **Resilience is a strategic process.** We are focusing on how operational resilience is a key contributor to an organization. It includes planning for, responding to, and recovering and benefiting from risks, significant business-impacting events, and crises. By acting on opportunities encountered during risks, events, and crises, resilience can become your competitive advantage.
- **Resilience is a value-added effect, not strictly a cost to your business.** A focus on long-term value over short-term efficiency may be a non-traditional concept for many, yet it is embraced by resilient organizations.
- **Resilience applies to all functions in your operations.** It is essential that the applicable functions embrace the concept since they are all contributors to a successful resilient process.

Socrates is quoted as saying "The more I know, the more I realize I know nothing".[1] He was a philosopher who realized the need for cross-functional dialogue in having a common understanding. He was an early generation resilience leader. As you gain experience, you may believe you have seen it all and are prepared for any risk, but you may have more than a few surprises waiting for you. We learned quite a bit from recent events like infectious disease outbreaks, wars and invasions, supply chain interruptions, cyber/ransomware effects, and natural incidents. Our organizations cannot operate in a vacuum. Every local crisis can quickly escalate to one that is national or global in scope. Every facility-based crisis can lead to one affecting your community and society in general. Every significant event will instantly be shared via global networks and social media. This recent cultural shift has helped to promote the value of a resilient organization. Be mindful that every action of a company has a domino effect. Examples of this cultural shift include your investor's focus on evolving environment, social, and governance norms.

Resilience Toolbox

If you start from scratch, attaining operational resilience can seem an insurmountable goal. However, the initial actions, documents, and tools that can help with your operational resilience journey are common to, and can be applied across, all sectors and lines of business. In this chapter we will assess what tools are viewed as providing value for building operational resilience in any organization. We will expand upon these concepts and illustrate examples in later chapters but will define and add them to your roadmap checklist now. Some of the concepts I've used to build and improve on resilience-based activities can be a great deal of value to you. Consider modifying the actions and tools shown below as you begin or improve your own process.

In this chapter we will review the following concepts tied to our roadmap, journey, and toolbox:

- Resilience Policy
- Organizational Charter
- Building a Project Plan
- Scorecard
- Blocks of Work
- Continuous Improvement

Resilience Policy

An operational resilience policy includes information and objectives that you will use to assess whether your operations are ready for, can recover from, and improve after a significant impact to your organization. It can include standards and guidelines that will be enforced to ensure resilience-based activities are well executed. Relevant policies will vary by organization and industry type. They are not one size fits all and may need to be updated from time to time. Changes in technologies and business risks can be contributors to policy revisions and updates. If the operational resilience policy is well written and defined, the organization can have well-aligned expectations for success. Some policies refer to business continuity management while others reference financial integrity.

The difference between a policy and a plan is in the details provided. They serve different purposes for your operations. The policy outlines standards and indicators to be met. It is the destination in your roadmap. The plan defines the entire journey that will be taken and includes details on how to reach the destination. The policy statement can be a single page referencing the components listed above, or it can be a more defined and detailed document which includes some of the additional concepts set forth below.

The following components can be part of your organizational resilience policy:

Introduction

Consider what your operations entail, what its mission is, and who is involved. The organization's annual report is a valuable reference to draw from to ensure there is a parallel between the organization's goals and how operational resilience will be attained. Include a reference to the mission, the stakeholders, risks, and responsibilities. A reference to planning for, responding to, and recovering from incidents, risks, and crises is also applicable.

Policy Statement/Summary

This statement sets forth the commitment to resilience across the organization. It can reference interactions between other relevant policies and programs already in place to help meet common goals. Consider adding references to how resilience contributes to your operational objectives in support of your associates and business operations. Specify who is managing the resilience process, how it is being implemented, and who will benefit from it.

Vision and Scope

The vision of the organization's resilience policy is a statement on what you want to accomplish through a well developed and implemented organizational resilience process. You can also reference the organization's mission. The scope of the policy should identify what activities are included and who is involved. All of the pertinent functions that are contributors to the mission can be referenced, including business continuity management, crisis management, incident response, supply chain, IT, and your security programs.

Definitions

Include clearly defined terms to be used where you suspect there may be a lack of clarity.

Ownership and Structure

Identify the groups or teams in the organization and include specific actions to help support resilience goals. A governance committee provides executive-level oversight, strategic direction, and the ability to navigate through operational resilience challenges. A global or strategic level leadership team manages the implementation of the governance committee's strategic direction. They should be aware of and engage with all global tactical functions and regionally based operational teams. Tactical team members execute actions to accomplish goals. They are subject matter experts in their field and know who to engage and the actions to take to meet resilience-based objectives. The operational resilience plan should include the composition of teams, the appropriate responsibilities, and relevant instructions for each team and function.

Compliance

Identify actions that are needed to be compliant with your policy and steps to be taken if exceptions occur. Evaluate and reference relevant industry standards and requirements that apply to your organization. Investigate how they also relate to your customers, suppliers, local governments, and communities.

Communicating the Policy

Clarify where the organizational resilience policy document will be located and how it will be communicated. It can be included with other resilience-focused documents that are shared with customers, suppliers, investors, and the public. I highly recommend closely aligning with your communications and legal teams on any documents that will be shared externally.

Organizational Charter

Your organizational resilience charter helps expand on the ownership of the resilience policy across your operations. It should reference appropriate governance actions based on your company's structure and culture. The right executive level stakeholders who are critical to operational success should be included in the charter. The charter helps to better define and document the overall team's objectives, resources, and constraints tied to your policy. Having an organizational charter is critical when forming a new governance committee or team and can also help to reenergize an existing governance team that has been in place for a long time.

Consider adding references to the following organizational charter components which are closely tied to your organizational resilience policy.

1. Form a Governance Process and Committee to prepare for, respond to, and recover from incidents, crises, and events that can adversely affect your organization.

2. Tie the policy to all business units and facilities that are part of the organization.
3. Identify the primary components of the charter and policy, including engaging your team, managing the resilience process, and maintaining and exercising plans and strategies.
4. Reference benchmarking to help promote continuous improvement and alignment with applicable standards and regulations.
5. Include how the overall operational resilience teams will be structured and what value they provide.
6. Document relevant actions integral to resilience planning, so present and future teams and stakeholders are aware of expectations and necessary commitments.

Building a Project Plan

In order to have an effective project management method or process, you must know how to identify goals, constraints, and deliverables over a specified time span. It's also important to include budget-related references for a common understanding of cost impacts. Factors that could both support and hinder operational resilience need to be referenced in your plan. A variety of tools and resources to help you identify timelines and goals are available. They include cloud-based applications, software, spreadsheets, and documents which will help simplify the execution of your plan and provide clarity across your organization. Once selected, the tools you use can be the primary method of tracking your team's resilience-based journey. Below are a few project planning concepts which are covered in greater detail in Chapters 5 and 6 of this book.

Long-Term Planning

Long-term planning is an effective way to engage multiple stakeholders and get them aligned on a common vision. Goals that take a long time to reach and that have many steps will be included in long-term planning. Consider including strategic goals you want to achieve in a three- to five-year time span. These goals should be closely tied to the organization's policy and scope. The documentation of this vision can help you break down objectives into manageable tasks over a defined time frame. This in turn will help you solve challenging problems by communicating effectively and eliminating roadblocks as they are discovered. Another benefit of documenting the vision is that it helps you make decisions on how to best use available resources in the most effective way. Once your planning is put into action, the key initiatives can be broken down into regular tasks, monitored, and adjusted as needed.

Shorter-Term Strategic Priorities (Tied to Long-Term Planning)

Shorter-term strategic priorities are key mid-term objectives which are targeted for the immediate two-year time span. They are part of the organization's long-term planning and are defined in a way that allows for adjustments to be made in the short term if necessary.

Immediate Strategic Priorities (Tied to Long-Term Planning)

Your immediate strategic priorities are the activities and actions for the upcoming year. They are clearly defined and support shorter- and long-term objectives, goals, and measures.

Short-Term Objectives (Tied to Immediate Strategic Priorities)

Your short-term objectives are defined actions that will be taken to attain immediate strategic priorities. **George T. Doran**[2] reportedly came up with the term SMART objectives in 1981. Since then, the acronym has been adapted to objective planning in different ways. SMART is generally understood to be defined as being:

- Specific: A specific objective is clearly defined, not vague, and easily understood.
- Measurable: A measurable objective identifies either quantitative or qualitative goals.
- Achievable: An achievable objective forms a common understanding between relevant parties on what the agreement shall be.
- Relevant: A relevant objective has beneficial meaning to the organization so when it is delivered, it will help overall performance.
- Time Bound: A time bound objective includes the time frame for completing each task with alignment on what success looks like.

Strengths, Weaknesses, Opportunities, Threats (SWOT) Analysis (Tied to Short-Term Objectives)

The SWOT framework[3] is credited to Albert Humphrey, who developed the approach at the Stanford Research Institute in the 1960s. A SWOT analysis is an excellent way to identify the organization's strategic resilience planning. SWOT analyses can assess internal and external factors, as well as current and future potential issues. It is a realistic and fact-based way to look at the strengths and weaknesses of an organization. It helps to eliminate opinions and establish facts that are accurate.

Let's review components of SWOT which we will also reference in future chapters of this book.

- Strengths can include internal factors you believe provide an advantage over your competitors. They can include services provided or products produced you believe are of significance.
- Weaknesses are internal factors creating a competitive disadvantage for your organization. Actions to take to minimize their impacts will then be identified.
- Opportunities should include the external actions you can focus on to be more effective and resilient. By executing well to these opportunities, you will attain greater success and they can become your strengths.
- Threats can include external factors that could create a significant negative effect on your operations. By identifying and planning for these risks, you are proactively working to minimize potential impacts on your operations, potentially creating an advantage over your competitors.

Scorecard

A scorecard is a management tool used to measure performance. The "balanced scorecard"[4] was originally developed by Dr. Robert Kaplan at Harvard University and Dr. David Norton in 1992 as a framework for measuring organizational performance. We reference it as a way of identifying and viewing strategic measures to get a more balanced view of performance to the organization's objectives. One of the many benefits of the balanced scorecard is that it gives you the ability to align the various components of strategic planning and management. It creates a better-defined connection between the objectives tied to various levels of planning in your scorecard. Key Performance Indicators (KPIs) were originally believed to be created by emperors of the Chinese Wei Dynasty[5] in the third century for rating performance of their extended family members. In the 1990s, Peter Drucker[6] identified the concept of performance indicators to give organizations a better way to understand the progress teams make on key business goals on a regular basis instead of learning it at the end. Developing KPIs aligned with your scorecard is of great value in your journey toward resilience. The KPIs tracked should match up with and support near-term objectives as defined in your project planning process. Your KPIs can be both quantitative and qualitative in nature. Quantitative KPIs can reference successful execution of objectives at a defined time by a defined group. Qualitative KPIs can include results of successfully executed events in support of resilience.

Blocks of Work

A very good way to track expected and actual time commitments toward resilient goals is by documenting your "blocks of work". We will share an example of what this looks like in later chapters of this book. The following steps help you document and maintain your blocks of work:

- Create a spreadsheet to track all activities.
- Include expected time commitments for activities to be taken by individuals or teams throughout the month and the year to reach resilience goals.
- Include alignment meetings as well as training and process improvement related activities.
- Include what's expected in preparing for, responding to, and improving upon business continuity events and crises.
- Consider including deliverables for each activity, showing their value-added impact.
- Compare the hours needed to complete everything expected of you with your available hours.

  - Your available time should not exceed 80 percent of the total hours you are expected to work in a year since an additional 20 percent is allotted for unforeseen activities and events requiring your participation.
  - Your available time is typically 40 hours per week times 52 weeks per year with a deduction for holidays and vacation time.

- Identify whether the commitments you are making cannot be reasonably accomplished in the allotted time; and if so, develop a modified plan.
- Reach out to your operational leadership for support needed to attain your original goals, or scale back to agreed-upon modified objectives with reasonable time commitments throughout the year.

Continuous Improvement (CI)

The "Plan, Do, Check, Act"[7] continuous improvement model is credited to William Deming. Most organizations use some form of it or at least understand its origin and value. Through origins in "Kaizen", "Six Sigma", and "Lean", it has become a cornerstone of how business operates, and it is critical to success in resilience. Once your teams complete their management of each incident, crisis, or business continuity event, you have an opportunity to assess gaps in planning and execution. By closing these gaps and building the lessons learned into future planning, you have taken steps to be better prepared and more resilient across your operations. We will share examples of CI activities in later chapters. For now, assess how CI is presently used in your organization and take steps to effectively improve upon planning and execution of resilience-related activities.

How to Lead, Follow and Guide the Way

Here are the key concepts to research and be ready to use throughout your Organizational Resilience Journey:

Develop a Roadmap

Know that it will be a journey executing a strategic process. It will require a great deal of time and commitment from cross-functional organizational teams. Important roadmap components include developing and improving upon your plan as well as focusing on the right behaviors to gain consensus.

Identify What's in Your Toolbox

Include the following resilience-based tools:

- Policy, Purpose, and Charter documents tying to the entire organization.
- Project Plan including long-term, immediate, and short-term strategic objectives.
- Scorecard referencing qualitative and quantitative KPIs.
- Blocks of Work summary to identify reasonable timeframes to execute objectives.

Keep focused on Continuous Improvement

Know there are opportunities to assess what's underway, identify gaps, and improve upon present resilience-based planning.

How to Lead

Develop your roadmap, visualize it, conceptualize it, and document the steps on your journey. Gather information on what you will use and how you will use it. Include the resilience-based tools that will blend in with your organization.

How to Follow

Be prepared to obtain feedback from subject matter experts in your organization and from those you've benchmarked with. Benchmarked means you have compared your program against others in similar organizations or with those programs considered world class or best in class. Modify your roadmap based on what you see as being of value to your team.

How to Guide the Way

- Begin to understand you have aligned your stakeholders and teams toward common goals, objectives, and measures as defined in your roadmap.
- Stay consistently focused on tracking feedback from teams with common goals.
- Make use of their knowledge and learn from their successes and mistakes.
- Look for the right timing to engage those who have that common vision.
- Eliminate complexity as you develop clarity by communicating easily understood goals.
- Get the right balance between what may be too much or too little.
- Let everyone know you value their input and that the process is team based and jointly developed and build on the energy created with your team.
- Continue to modify your roadmap and remain focused on continuous improvement.

Notes

1 https://www.thecollector.com/all-i-know-is-that-i-know-nothing-socrates/
2 George T. Doran, 'There's a S.M.A.R.T. way to write management's goals and objectives', AMA Forum, https://community.mis.temple.edu/mis0855002fall2015/files/2015/10/S.M.A.R.T-Way-Management-Review.pdf
3 Teoli D, Sanvictores T, An J. SWOT Analysis. [Updated 2022 Sep 5]. In: Stat-Pearls [Internet]. Treasure Island (FL): StatPearls Publishing; 2023 Jan-. Available from: https://www.ncbi.nlm.nih.gov/books/NBK537302/
4 Robert S. Kaplan and David P. Norton, 'Putting the Balanced Scorecard to Work', Harvard Business Review, September-October 1993, https://hbr.org/1993/09/putting-the-balanced-scorecard-to-work
5 Zahra Currimbhoy, 'The Ultimate KPI Guide', https://www.perdoo.com/kpi-guide/#:~:text=While%20the%20exact%20origin%20of,performance%20of%20the%20royal%20family.
6 https://bluecallom.com/peter-drucker/
7 https://www.lean.org/lexicon-terms/pdca/#:~:text=PDCA%20is%20an%20improvement%20cycle,in%20Japan%20in%20the%201950s.

Chapter III

Turning Risk into Opportunity

You've taken some major steps to either develop a new organizational resilience program or improve an existing one. Evaluating pockets of expertise to help support your team to follow a common roadmap is an important
initial first step. We've identified some of the tools you can use to help
clearly define your strategy roadmap and how you will ultimately deploy
it. Your resilience toolbox will include a policy, purpose, charter, project
plan, scorecard, blocks of work, and continuous improvement documents,
plans, and tools. They all help to maximize the probability of your success.
The next step is determining how well risk is understood, reported, and
managed across your operations.

Risk is defined as a possible event that has both positive and negative
implications. When you mention the word "risk" to someone, their immediate reaction could be negative. A negative reaction is likely based
upon knowing risk is a possible event or threat that could cause negative
impacts to your operations, including an inability to achieve your objectives. This perception is accurate, yet there is another way to look at risk.
When you effectively manage risks, you create opportunities for improvement. Based on the level of improvement gained, you can turn the management of risk into a competitive advantage. Effective management of risk
can help attract more customers and grow market share when it's obvious
you managed a major incident or crisis well when your competitors did
not.

In this chapter we will review the following risk-related concepts:

- Common Risks Turned into Opportunities
- Enterprise Risk Management (ERM) as an Opportunity
- Incident Reporting as an Opportunity
- Additional Common Risks
- Unexpected (Novel) Risks
- Identifying Your Top Operational Risks
- Overcoming Fear of Reporting of Incidents and Risks

DOI: 10.4324/9781003438700-3

Common Risks Turned into Opportunities

We will review some examples of how a resilient organization can use common risks as an opportunity to gain competitive advantage. These risks could also have major negative operational and financial impacts if not managed effectively. We will expand on the opportunities and benefits created from them and other risks in greater detail in chapters that follow.

Supply Chain Risk

Risk: A primary risk for every manufacturer is to rely on critical materials from a sole source supplier, meaning that this supplier is the only supplier (source) that can deliver a required product to the manufacturer. A risk that affects a sole source supplier may have a significant impact on your ability to produce a product and meet the needs of your customers. We are all exposed to potential risks like severe weather, facility breakdowns, ransomware issues, and ID outbreaks. Any of these can occur and create a facility closure for your sole source critical material supplier. Their exposure to a variety of local human, natural, or technological events or incidents can quickly make them unable to manufacture or deliver contractually committed materials. If this occurs when you have a limited supply of their product during a critical production time, you may be unable to meet your obligations and customers' requirements. Their inability to provide you with materials can result in your organization being exposed to contractual penalties and loss of market share with immediate financial and reputational effects.

Opportunity: The simple answer to manage sole source supplier risk is to have no single or sole source suppliers. That sounds a lot simpler than it is, as there may be times when you develop a new product that requires a material that can only be sourced from one location. Being aware of the resilience of your single or sole source supplier is a priority. Consider conducting robust risk assessments of their operations and include second and third tier suppliers that help support them. A risk that has a major impact on primary, secondary, or third tier suppliers can affect you significantly. It's common practice to survey critical suppliers with risk-based questions that reveal the extent of their planning for significant risks.

Another effective way of assessing the health of your critical suppliers is to conduct on-site audits of their facilities to identify potential issues that could affect you. Base the audit questions on their potential exposure to common risks. Evaluate their facility with as much detail as you would your own and summarize your audit findings. Consider providing solutions to any audit findings since they may help minimize negative impacts to their operations which also benefit you. You may be taking steps your competitors are not, thereby turning this risk into opportunity and gaining a substantial advantage over them.

Natural Incident Risk

Risk: Regardless of location, we are all exposed to geographically based risks. Common risks include hurricanes, typhoons, tornadoes, flooding, and earthquakes. You are likely aware of natural risks if they've previously caused significant impact to your operations. However, because significant damage from natural incidents may not occur very often, complacency can set in. Although you know damages can be significant, you tend to focus on other significant present-day challenges. Nevertheless, a significant naturally based incident has the ongoing potential to affect your associates and their families, the community, and business operations.

Opportunity: Consider developing a proactive process to maintain awareness on both high probability and high impact locally based natural incidents. Communicate regularly with your associates on how they can prepare for natural incidents at home with their families, schools, and communities. Prepare your facilities for potential impacts from natural risks. Identify potential gaps in your planning and gain operational support on implementing solutions for these risks. Doing so increases the probability that your associates and business operations will be better prepared to respond to and recover quickly from natural incident-based risks.

ID Risk

Risk: COVID-19, multiple Covid variants, and other recent ID outbreaks have proven to be one of the greatest risks affecting humanity in our generation. Far-reaching effects from ID outbreaks include the health of our workers, behavioral impact on society in general, and significant unforeseen costs to maintain operations. Government mandates had a major effect on how citizens traveled, worked, and behaved. Changes to our daily routines became the norm. Our business priorities included protecting our people and operations from ID outbreaks. This was likely the lengthiest combined personal and business event most of us ever experienced.

Opportunity: We learned significant lessons from how we managed impacts from COVID-19 and variants in the past few years. New protocols were developed for keeping people safe and healthy. New methods of working and engaging cross-functional teams became commonplace. By developing an ID playbook, you can capture key actions and lessons learned from this significant global pandemic. A playbook is a document that consolidates your organization's successfully executed activities in response to an outbreak. Include references to the protocols, policies, and procedures your operations successfully implemented. By keeping the playbook technically current and available, you bypass significant time needed to redevelop and redeploy them. Consider conducting tests of your ID plans from time to time to increase awareness and improve future effectiveness of your playbook.

Lack of Talent (Workers) Risk

Risk: When it comes to resilience-based activities, every role on your team is critical. A single individual who is unable to effectively execute a task can cause a critical path gap in your team's success. A competitive marketplace for workers combined with an aging workforce makes it tough to find and retain employees. A standard 40-hour work week and a "doing whatever it takes to get the job done" attitude has changed. Workers today value their personal time, and a "work to live" mentality has taken priority over "live to work." Customary job descriptions and expectations of our workers may not work anymore.

Opportunity: You are making a significant commitment to being more resilient by being aware of your most critical job functions and identifying and training alternate team members. A resilient organization recognizes the way it recruits and how it retains its associates and that significantly contributes to the organization's success. Be proactive by conducting frequent surveys of your associates and be responsive to their needs. This creates a proactive worker partnership which leads to competitive advantage. Social media also plays a key role in effectively communicating your values and commitments to your workers.

Facility and Infrastructure Failure Risk

Risk: We've reviewed the significant role critical suppliers have in your operations. They may also present a major risk to your operations. You should also consider the importance of your own facilities in supporting your ability to maintain market share and meet the needs of your customers. Any incident that can cause your facilities to close for an extended period of time can have both an immediate and long-term negative impact. Examples of facility-related issues that can make your operations nonproductive include failure of critical equipment, facility fires, and property damage.

Opportunity: Proactive property protection along with well-executed human element programs at your most critical locations help operational resilience. Your risk management, safety, and environmental teams and insurers can provide guidance on steps to take to minimize significant facility-related risks. Human element programs are those that do not have significant cost impact and require actions rather than capital to be effective. They can be a major contributor in minimizing damage and cost impact from risks. Various human element actions create an effective way to speed up recovery from facility-related incidents. Reliability is a term used to describe expected equipment performance for a defined time. A formal reliability program can help to maintain equipment effectively and avoid unexpected breakdowns or lack of optimal performance. The end result is that your facility operates as expected.

By identifying the most important operational risks that could affect your operations, you've taken another step to support your resilience strategy. This provides the framework for effectively managing these risks. During this initial risk assessment process, consider how you can quickly get support, build, or improve upon your overall resilience strategy. Assess whether there are any effective programs already in place involving your Risk Management or ERM teams. Does your organization already have a clear, well understood, and standardized way of identifying and quantifying risk? If so, you are off and running. If not, consider developing an ERM process as many progressive organizations have done. Key considerations of an ERM process are highlighted below. These concepts will align with resilient deployment planning in later chapters.

Enterprise Risk Management (ERM) As an Opportunity

Global organizations are interconnected—technologically, financially, economically, socially, and environmentally. Their interdependencies make risk landscapes more dynamic, with risks no longer clearly defined by traditional risk assessments. Many organizations rely on multiple departments and business units to identify, evaluate, and summarize risks. As a result, there may be a lack of transparency or consistency across the company in all applicable categories of risk.

Without an ERM process, an external perception may exist that management has not adequately identified all material risks that can impact your organization's cash flow, capital, and mission. Market and credit analysts may perceive your risk disclosure capabilities as not being "effectively strengthened". There may be a misconception that strategies are not in place for accurate and effective risk analysis across the organization. Risks may not be fully aligned with risk appetite, and steps may not be in place to leverage results to benefit the organization. You will not be able to reap the benefits of economies of scale with risk reporting since the components of an overall "risk register" are spread across many initiatives in your organization. By utilizing ERM, a comprehensive risk assessment is built into all business processes. This results in more efficient use of capital. Comprehensive risk profiles are reported and calculated risk taking is in place. Resources are channeled toward the highest growth and potential return areas. Losses are controlled more effectively. A consistent and targeted method of managing risk is enabled.

Below are a steps to consider when forming a new ERM committee or team:

1. Obtain support in the form of an interested and engaged "risk champion" at the senior leadership team level.
2. Secure any funding needed to get started.
3. Ensure that it is a companywide process that accurately tracks and manages all risks.
4. Include Business Continuity, Risk Management, Internal Audit, IT, Security, and Finance in your initial ERM Committee, adding other teams as needed.
5. Align with your industry accepted risk standards, practices, activities, and elements.
6. Determine which software-based tool will be used and who will contribute to the consolidated risk summary.
7. Establish a regular cadence for reporting and management of risks.
8. Maintain consistency in terminology to support appropriate actions including accountability, repeatability, and reporting.
9. Consider a quarterly cadence of risk discussions by your committee.
10. Encourage the organization to actively track risks and not "punish" those who are involved in risk reporting.

Opportunity: A single consistent method to identify, measure, evaluate, and manage risks and seize opportunities provides benefits for your organization. Having a common framework for risk management includes

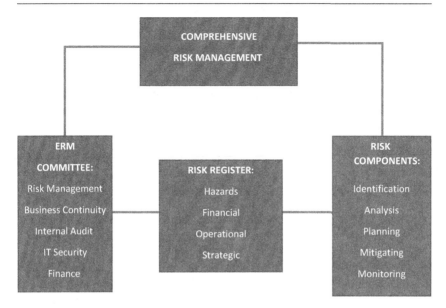

Figure 3.1 ERM components.

identifying risks and opportunities along with assessing their likelihood and impact. This provides a consistent way to determine a response strategy and monitor progress. This is a clear component of resilience in creating value for stakeholders, including your associates, customers, shareholders, and society overall.

With ERM effectively in place, a risk aware culture exists at all levels. A dedicated risk committee with cross-functional representation is a low cost and high potential impact process to consider if you have none. See Figure 3.1 for a comprehensive ERM overview.

Upcoming chapters will include additional insight into how to tie relevant risk to resilient deployment.

Incident Reporting as an Opportunity

Does your organization know the difference between *risks* and *incidents*? It may surprise you that many organizations mistakenly use the terms interchangeably. It's important to understand the terms and use them correctly so your organization can better understand their risks and the steps needed to enact mitigation actions. Let's agree on a common definition we will use to help define differences between incidents and risks so that you can use them more effectively throughout your organization.

Risks Defined

A risk is the *potential (or likelihood) that something bad may happen. It can also be an event that may cause harm, create a loss, or stop you from meeting specified objectives. A risk creates potential loss for your organization.* The execution of inadequate or failed procedures and controls can also be tied to operational risks.

Incidents Defined

An incident is *when something bad has happened.* You may not know immediately if an incident will create a loss; however, it involves some sort of negative event that is tied to a risk.

A basic concept we've reviewed is the need to have a common understanding of how to report incidents in an organization along with a common language to ensure clarity in reporting and effectively managing the incidents afterwards. Misconceptions involving what an incident, crisis, disaster, and bad thing is require clarification. Does your organization classify different levels of crises? Is it overly complicated and not aligned with the goal to keep concepts simple and better understood? Let's consider a common way of referring to risks affecting your operations in this book. A few of the related terms we will use along with their definitions are shared below.

Major and Minor Incidents

A major incident is an event that may cause significant impact to your operations. Consider how you can formalize what a major incident is and how it will be reported across your organization. A major incident policy with an ongoing communications plan can help. Major incidents which have significant operational impacts can include:

- Any fatality of your associates, contractors, or visitors on site or in a work-related setting.
- Multiple injuries to associates, contractors, or visitors.
- An event that shuts down your operations for more than a single shift of production or business-related activity.
- The presence of law enforcement or similar government authorities on site in any of your facilities.
- Negative media coverage of your operations.
- Activities affecting your operations that can affect your organization's reputation or can cause significant penalties or fines.
- Environmental releases (air, land, or water) above the governmentally approved reportable limit.

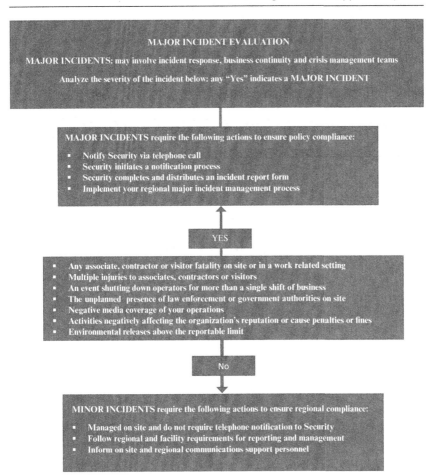

Figure 3.2 Major incident evaluation.

Minor incidents are incidents not significant enough in scale or those that do not have as big of an impact as the major incidents referenced above. See the flow chart in Figure 3.2 that details how to evaluate an incident and suggests actions to take.

Major Incident Policy

Consider developing a major incident reporting policy to ensure there is clarity on expectations across your organization. The policy should pertain to your entire organization and have appropriate legal, communications, and operational leadership approval. Let's also agree upon a common way to have anyone in your organization report major incidents. If you have a security function that is active and available around the clock, consider having them be the department that manages the initial reporting of incidents in your organization. They can maintain a contact list to use for making initial notifications when incidents are reported. Security can notify the operational team impacted by the major incident as the first step. The operational team can implement business continuity or crisis management activities to minimize operational impacts. If additional escalation is needed, corporate or global team members can aid as well. Following chapters in this book will include examples of how to effectively manage a business continuity event when an incident escalates to the point of creating business impact. Various mass notification tools (e.g., software and apps) are available to help in the notification process. Be aware of privacy laws in various countries that dictate how you obtain phone numbers and emails for those who will be contacted and how you must protect private information from unauthorized access.

Opportunity: Having a common way to report major incidents allows the organization to accurately identify them and begin an effective response. Time is a critical factor in deploying the resources needed to speed up recovery, minimize business interruptions and avoid unnecessary expenses. Documenting and tracking the major incidents by category, type, and duration will help you identify what preemptive measures should be taken in the future. These avoidance measures can relate to human elements or require capital expenditures. They play a role in minimizing business interruptions and are a contributor to effective organizational risk management.

Additional Common Risks

Identifying the most obvious risks in an organization is an initial step. It is easily understood but can be difficult to accurately complete due to competing priorities in various departments. We have covered the business value of an ERM process. If you do not have one in place, see what components you do have and align strategies to them with an ultimate vision of implementing an ERM process. The obvious operational risks include those that are a combination of incidents reported and actual business continuity events you have managed. The differences between incidents, crises, and business continuity events will be covered later. For now, we will consider the combination of risks and incidents the organization has experienced. You will likely be asked, "When did that last happen here?" Be better prepared for that question by having concrete examples of incidents your teams have handled. Here are a few significant risks for you to consider and make part of your overall risk-based decision making:

Supply Chain Risks

Supply chain risks include the combination of sourcing of materials (e.g., raw materials for manufacturing) and the logistics and transportation to source, produce, and deliver them to your customers. Recent global issues have contributed to supply chain risks being included in many organizations' top risks due to several factors. Our global economy prior to and after the recent COVID-19 pandemic created volatility and uncertainty, including fears of a global recession. Manufacturers' inability to increase inventories to maintain steady supply contributed to supply chain risk. Your suppliers' abilities to maintain performance and their financial health are very common risks. Financial sanctions also play a key role in supply chain volatility. It is important to know who your suppliers' owners, shareholders, and directors are in case financial sanctions are mandated by governments. Planning for customer demand was complicated due to changes in buying patterns as COVID-19 confined people to their homes. This introduced pent-up demand which companies could not always easily plan for. In addition, the global labor shortage made it more difficult and at times seemingly impossible to hire workers with the skills needed to step right in and support resilience activities. This affected suppliers' abilities to produce a product or deliver a service on time. Additionally, high inflation created unexpected price increases affecting your organization's ability to meet their operating plan. This resulted in substantial unexpected costs for most organizations.

Natural Incidents (e.g., floods, typhoons, earthquakes, extreme temperatures, etc.)

Natural hazards (risks) are defined by **FEMA**[1] as environmental phenomena that can impact society and human environment. They may cause loss of life, injury, or other health impacts, property damage, loss of livelihoods and services, social and economic disruption, or environmental damage. They are described by their magnitude or intensity, speed of onset, duration, and area of extent. For example, earthquakes have short durations and usually affect a relatively small region, whereas droughts are slow to develop and fade away and often affect large regions. In some cases, hazards may be coupled, as is the case with a flood caused by a hurricane or a tsunami that is created by an earthquake. Natural risks are specific to geographical locations. You cannot escape them, so you must be prepared to respond to them.

Geopolitical Events (e.g., wars, violence, thefts, etc.)

Geopolitical risks have the potential to threaten the operational and financial stability and resilience of your organization. It is important to understand each organizational site's exposure to a variety of these risks. For our operational resilience-based evaluation, let's include war, civil unrest, and terrorism as components of this risk. They can increase tension between countries and affect the peaceful course of international relations.

Collective Bargaining Agreements (CBA) and Strike

A CBA is an agreed-upon and documented legal contract between your organization and the union representing your employees or associates. The CBA is the result of a well detailed negotiation process between both parties regarding critical topics such as wages, hours, and terms and conditions of employment. They also reference job health and safety policies, ways to balance work and family, and more. Collective bargaining normally takes place between members of corporate management and labor leaders who are elected by workers to represent them and their interests. Collective bargaining is initiated when employee contracts are up for renewal or when employers make changes to the workplace or contracts.

IT Resilience (e.g., applications, outlook, etc.)

To have IT resilience, you must have the ability to continuously keep essential operationally reliant IT infrastructure, systems, and applications up and running despite incidents, crises, disasters, and disruptions. You need to maintain acceptable levels of service and access, regardless of software or hardware failures. In addition, you need to have adequate capacity to deal with spikes in IT system demands and be proactive in managing trending issues that can cause outages and noncompliance. Security must be in place to prevent adverse effects from risks such as cyber issues and ransomware. A plan for quick response and recovery by appropriate teams is also part of being IT resilient. The recovery component includes maintaining active maintenance contracts for your hardware, having spare equipment and capacity, keeping backups of critical system configurations, and having a process in place to quickly validate system readiness.

Facility Impacts

Operational resilience of your building and facilities is required in order to allow your associates to conduct business. Potential issues with your facilities include fires, utility outages, and the lack of operational equipment and building systems. A sound strategy includes conducting a vulnerability assessment to determine how your facilities can withstand potential harm from internal and external sources. Following building codes which provide guidance on construction and ongoing management of building systems can help build resilience. Your insurers have recommendations on maintaining the location as a highly protected risk. They base their recommendations on impacts to similar structures and operations from others they insure and protect. Contributing factors for your facilities include upgrades to structures, better preventive maintenance, equipment reliability, and effective property protection system installations. Manufacturing and engineering teams are typically skilled at coordinating activities and maintenance strategies to reduce the risk and impacts of equipment failures.

Associate Injuries or Fatalities

Federal OSHA defines recommended practices designed to be used in all business settings. The Recommended Practices[2] present a step-by-step approach to implementing a safety and health program built around seven core elements that make up a successful program.

The main goal of safety and health programs is to prevent workplace injuries, illnesses, and deaths, as well as the suffering and financial hardship these events can cause for workers, their families, and employers. The recommended practices use a proactive approach to managing workplace safety and health. They recognise that finding and fixing hazards before they cause injury or illness is a far more effective approach. You should avoid traditional approaches which are often reactive—that is, problems are addressed only after a worker is injured or becomes sick, a new standard or regulation is published, or an outside inspection finds a problem that must be fixed.

If you're starting from scratch, begin with a basic safety program with simple goals and grow from there. If you focus on achieving goals, monitoring performance, and evaluating outcomes, your workplace can progress along a path to higher levels of safety and health achievement.

Employers will find that implementing these recommended practices also brings other benefits. Safety and health programs help businesses:

- **Prevent** workplace injuries and illnesses.
- **Improve** compliance with laws and regulations.
- **Reduce** costs, including significantly reducing workers' compensation premiums.
- **Engage** workers.
- **Enhance** their social responsibility goals.
- **Increase** productivity and enhance overall business operations.

Environmental Risks

The **US Environmental Protection Agency (EPA)**[3] considers environmental risk to be the chance of harmful effects to human health or to ecological systems resulting from exposure to an environmental issue. Various organizations agree on the following types of environmental risks:

- Air contaminants.
- Toxic waste.
- Radiation.
- Disease-causing microorganisms and plants.
- Pesticides.
- Heavy metals.
- Chemicals in consumer products.
- Extreme temperatures and weather events.

Anything that causes an exposure greater than a legally required reportable limit creates an environmental incident. It must be quickly reported and managed effectively to maintain operational resilience.

Unexpected (Novel) Risks

Novel is defined by Merriam Webster as something that is new, not resembling something formerly known, used, or previously defined[4]. The original COVID-19 outbreak in 2019 and Russia's invasion of Ukraine in 2022 would not have been considered obvious risks most organizations were planning for. You could consider them novel as defined by Webster.

Goodyear's ID planning had been in place for over a decade prior to COVID-19. We had already developed and communicated the benefits of ID planning. This included developing and deploying over a dozen different ID protocols throughout all our regions. Tabletop exercises were conducted to train all operational teams on actions with ID as the focal point. The exercises identified gaps which were turned into lessons learned. When COVID-19 became a global pandemic, Goodyear's teams implemented resilience-based actions quickly and effectively.

In a similar way, we were affected by multiple political conflicts in Latin America, Europe, Middle East, and Asia Pacific. By responding to incidents, crises, and business continuity events, we discovered gaps, improved on our readiness, and shared lessons learned across all our regions. We were well underway in planning for Russia's invasion in support of our associates and business operations.

Unexpected risks can include incidents others have experienced but your organization typically will not focus on. Consider benchmarking and

Table 3.1 Example of Operational Risks

Operational Risks with Potential for Organizational Impact

Conduct Risk	Human Capital Risk
Climate Change (Extreme)	Human Resource Errors
Crime and Violence	Infectious Disease
Cyber Risk	Infrastructure Failure
Data Theft and Misuse	Regulatory Risk
Digital Inadequacy	Strike, CBA Impacts
Environmental Impact	Supply Chain
Facility Unavailability	Utility Interruption
Fire and Explosion	Violence and Protests
Geopolitical	Weather and Nature

looking at business sectors different than yours when identifying unexpected risks. See what risks they are focused on that you may not be planning for.

Opportunity: As referenced earlier, local incidents can quickly escalate to national, then global levels. An incident or event can cause a ripple effect which ultimately affects your operations. Some unexpected risks and events may be outside your control. Both obvious and unexpected or novel risks can have a major impact on your business operations. These risks may materialize very quickly, on an enormous scale, impacting the entire world. A resilient organization will have thought through their response to any risk and how they can turn their response into an advantage. By planning a response to novel risks you're a step ahead of others who have not taken proactive steps.

See Table 3.1 for a summary of common operational risks to consider in your overall risk analysis.

Identifying Your Top Operational Risks

We've reviewed how a well-developed ERM process provides a common framework for identifying risks across an entire organization. The next step is assessing their likelihood and impact. You can turn risks into opportunities by being aware of both obvious and novel risks and building a resilience-based framework that takes them into account. You can have anywhere between four to six categories of risk across an organization. They can include health and safety, reputational, strategic, compliance, financial, and operational risks. Your next step is to identify your top operational risks. Let's review how the four factors below should all be considered when stating you've accurately identified your top operational risks:

1. Operational Risk Assessment Results
2. Major Incidents Affecting Your Operations
3. Unexpected (Novel) and Benchmarked Risks
4. Selecting Your "Top Operational Risks"

Operational Risk Assessment Results

Your risk assessment identified various risks affecting your organization. These risks likely include a broad category of risks. Some are the responsibility of other organizational teams who have expertise in managing them. Operational risks can never be fully eliminated or avoided. The organization must decide what level of operational risk assessment results it is comfortable accepting.

Major Incidents Affecting Your Operations

The next activity that contributes to selecting your top operational risks is tracking the actual incidents that have been reported and that have had an impact on your operations. An effective way to document them is through business continuity software or a simple spreadsheet which you can see in Table 3.2. Consider following a format to track reported incidents and that enables you to sort data as referenced below:

- The Region the incident originated in – This provides data on which region had the greatest need for support throughout the year. This can be of value to various operational teams.
- The exact location of the incident – You can then determine which location may need facility or human element attention to avoid similar incidents in the future.
- The date of the incident's occurrence – Add this in order to track them accurately.
- Category of the incident – This allows you to determine which type had the greatest impact to your operations overall. If you're consistently experiencing certain incidents (e.g., IT issues, natural incidents, or supply chain interruptions), you can justify spending capital funding on preventive measures or training on human element programs to minimize their impacts in the future.
- A brief description of the incident – This allows you to reference it more easily in the future.

Table 3.2 Global Incident Tracking

Global Tracking of Regional Major Incidents

Region of Origin (Select Region A, B, C or D)	Regional Location (City of origin)	Date Occurred (When it began)	Incident Type (General category)	Description of Incident (How it occurred and present status)	Duration Select < 1 day > 1 day > 1 week

- Duration of each incident – Consider documenting the duration for each incident so you can track which type required the greatest time commitment by your business continuity or crisis management team:

  o Less than one day: This can be the shortest time of engagement tracked for team response to mitigate the incident's effects through when you return to pre-incident mode.

  o Between one day and one week: The severity of the incident was enough to keep the team involved more than a day yet was resolved anywhere between the first day and the next few, under a total of seven days.

  o Greater than one week: The severity of incidents lasting more than a week have the greatest probability of having severe business impacts and of involving numerous team members to resolve them.

Unexpected (Novel) and Benchmarked Risks

Evaluate what unique risks have not been identified that have the potential to significantly affect your operations. Consider including novel risks that your customer, supplier, or benchmarked organization has experienced that caused them a significant business impact. Examples of recent risks considered novel were infectious disease, wars involving countries where your suppliers or customers are based, and ransomware events. Although they were known to be of significant potential concern, most organizations

Table 3.3 Top Operational Risks

Top Operational Risks Based on Analyses of:
1. **Annual Risk Assessment**
2. **Annual Regional Incident Tracking**
3. **Benchmarked and External References**

Natural Incidents: weather, natural based events, climatological trends
Facility and Infrastructure Failure: equipment or facility unavailability, reliability issues, fire
Supply Chain Issues: ongoing impacts of procuring and delivering products, second and third tier supplier and customer issues
IT Systems Impact: availability of equipment, systems, applications and concerns with potential cyber security and ransomware events
Geopolitical Risk: potential for war, protests, and violence affecting associates and business operations
Talent (People) Impact: availability of associates in critical roles, lack of bench strength, inadequate transition of knowledge across the organization

---

may not have spent a great deal of time planning for the risks and putting preventive actions in place. Remember that something considered to be unique today may become quite commonplace tomorrow.

Selecting the Top Operational Risks

Evaluate which operational risks have significant impact potential as identified in your risk assessment or ERM process. Compare them with actual incidents which have a high recent rate of occurrence or extended time of team engagement. Also consider novel risks which have the potential to severely impact your associates and business operations. Determine which of these risks you may not have effectively planned for. Every risk demands some type of planning and engagement to mitigate its effects. Alignment across your operations on "what matters most" from a risk perspective can be reviewed on an annual basis and modified as needed. See Table 3.3 as an example of top operational risks across an organization.

Overcoming Fear of Reporting Incidents and Risks

One of the first and most important actions in overall management of risk is accepting reality and overcoming the fear of reporting incidents and risks. Many of us are wired to avoid things we do not want to hear or see. Some of this is unconscious behavior. Some of it is the fear your management may be unforgiving if you unintentionally caused an incident, there will be repercussions and it will affect you personally, perhaps financially.

There's a great deal of work involved in effectively planning for risks. It's much easier to deny the possibility that we could have a pandemic shut down the entire world than to develop protocols, an infectious disease playbook and train your teams for infectious disease outbreaks. Similarly, it's easier to deny that a country will invade another one and plan for how to support your associates, prepare for interruptions to your critical material suppliers and look for alternatives in conducting business. A resilient organization encourages and embraces reporting of all incidents and risks. The quicker you're made aware of bad news, the quicker you can make appropriate decisions to either avoid them, manage them, or recover from them.

Here are a few goals for your operational teams to overcome fear of reporting incidents and risks:

1. Accepting bad news by developing a culture of supporting its reporting and taking what's reported into consideration and your decision making.
2. Avoiding public criticism when someone did something wrong or took the initiative to make you aware of what could be perceived as bad news.
3. Address the news, so it's obvious you support prompt reporting of any event that has occurred or could be an operational risk.
4. Applying feedback and expectations as part of a teaching moment when it's applicable.
5. Appropriate communication in support of reporting bad news should be shared in multiple ways. Your associates are aware of now only what's shared via email, policies, and procedures. Verbal, visual and listening communications deliver an important message regarding how you truly support reporting and management of bad news.

How to Lead, Follow & Guide the Way

Here are the steps to take to turn risks into opportunity and maintain resilient operations:

o **Consolidate all Risks** by gaining input from those with expertise who may presently be evaluating risks. Consider developing a single method of managing risks, such as an ERM process. Include both common and uncommon (novel) risks in the overall risk evaluation. Determine your top operational risks based on their potential likelihood and scope of impact.
o **Develop an Incident Reporting Policy** to identify and report major incidents consistently across your organization. Document major incidents

by category, type, and duration and develop preemptive measures to avoid them or minimize their impacts in the future.

How to Lead

Consider if an ERM process can be implemented in your organization. Evaluate how incidents are being reported and managed. See how actual events and crises are also being reported and managed. Look for consistency across the organization. Find gaps and opportunities for improvement. Assess trending risks applicable to your organization. Be prepared to supplement this with the unexpected risks that may not be applicable now, yet other sectors and businesses seem to be "all in" on.

How to Follow

Align with others who may have components of an ERM process underway. Use current terminology that is aligned with industry standards for risk-based decision making. Develop a common risk tracking method across your organization with an agreed upon timeframe for updating all risks.

How to Guide the Way

Establish and maintain a vision on the long-term benefits of a well-developed risk-based decision-making process. Adjust what the structure and deliverables should be based on where you have pockets of expertise in your organization. Provide awareness and training on the major incident reporting policy and process. Use incorrect reporting of incidents as a teaching moment to gain support throughout your operations. Focus on the top operational risks and make necessary adjustments to all other risks by having a consistent method to manage common and novel risks. Encourage immediate reporting of incidents and risks without instilling fear or retaliation to those who report it.

Notes

1 https://hazards.fema.gov/nri/natural-hazards#:~:text=Natural%20 hazards%20are%20defined%20as,hazards%2C%20such%20as%20 manmade%20hazards
2 Occupational Safety and Health Administration, 'Recommended Practices for Safety and Health Programs', https://www.osha.gov/safety-management/step-by-step-guide
3 https://www.epa.gov/
4 https://www.merriam-webster.com/dictionary/novel

Chapter IV

Aligning Your Teams

Your operational resilience journey is well underway. You've done research and formed the framework and overall resilience structure. You're getting aligned with those in key roles who will support alignment across your operations. You've developed the policy and organizational charter. Your project plan will help set attainable short- and long-term objectives. Your scorecard will help track objectives as you monitor progress toward key performance targets. You will document the time commitments needed to address foreseen and unforeseen activities through your blocks of work analysis. Common tasks and goals can be executed in a reasonable time frame. The most critical objectives can be reprioritized, or you can seek additional help if needed. Risk-based decision making will be understood across all levels of your organization. A review of your operational risk summary, the actual incidents you've tracked, and your novel risk considerations will help to identify your top operational risks. An accurate and effective risk management strategy will be in place.

What's your next step? You now need to look at your organization to determine which critical roles need to be included on your team. You can then form the right structure for a team-based approach to proactively address and support operational resilience. This is a great time to reflect on the importance of teamwork in operational resilience. A recent study by **Yale University**[1] identified teamwork as an essential skill to help us accomplish organizational goals and objectives. Their study included five reasons why teamwork is important:

1. A team environment allows individuals to bring their diverse perspectives to problem solving, which in turn increases their success at arriving at solutions more efficiently and effectively.
2. When the whole team works as a unit, everyone has an opportunity to learn from each other. This process leads to resource building and enables the team to become better equipped to deal with new challenges.

DOI: 10.4324/9781003438700-4

3. Teamwork can improve efficiency and productivity when responsibilities are shared and project timelines are successfully addressed.
4. Teamwork can be effective in building great working relationships.
5. **Teamwork brings an expanded sense of accomplishment. When people perform as one unit, they can exceed individual achievements.**

In this chapter we will review the following team-based concepts to support operational resilience:

- Organizational Assessment
- Governance Committee Team and Charter
- Global Business Continuity Team Structure
- Regional Business Continuity Team Alignment
- Tactical and Facility Operational Support
- Operational Incident Response
- Business Continuity Events
- Crisis Management Team
- Cross Functional Coordination
- Dynamic Execution

Organizational Assessment

An effective way to structure, align, and create balance with all your teams starts with an accurate understanding of your organization's global presence. Let's use the term global to define all business units that are part of the organization throughout the world. It has different connotations for small, medium, and large companies. A small company with facilities in a single state or country is much more centralized than a multinational one with facilities and associates in many countries. Publicly traded companies have a well-defined structure. Their strategies, products, and goals are highlighted on their corporate website.

When structuring your teams, consider aligning them with your operational functions. Start building your teams in alignment with the organizational framework that's identified in your company's mission and review how they will support the strategies defined on your corporate website. This allows a functional approach in an organization of any size. It keeps all teams better focused in supporting their respective goals to provide a safe workplace for your associates, improve performance of your business, unlock new business opportunities, and manage risks more effectively. Your investor relations site provides valuable insight into your company's financial commitments with majority shareholders. The commitments are updated through quarterly earnings reports.

Benchmarking the team structure of other companies can also help validate that you are on the right path. Check the team structure of your customers, suppliers, competitors, and other world-class organizations. Determine whether you share common industry-based compliance standards which will be supported well by your proposed team structure.

Governance Committee Team and Charter

Effective governance of your operational resilience process allows you to act in the best interests of the organization. A committee approach to making strategic decisions is most beneficial. This approach creates value by including diverse perspectives from those with a great deal of relevant leadership experience. It can improve business decision making, maintain stability, improve productivity, and create business opportunities. The governance committee's role is to support strategic decision making throughout the organization. They are skilled at prioritized risk-based decision making. A governance team structure should include leaders at the highest level of the organization in critical roles tied to the risks, incidents, and activities related to them. The senior executives on the governance committee will champion the operational resilience process by setting strategies, objectives and the agreed upon project framework.

Governance Committee Team Members

See Table 4.1 for an example of a governance committee structure with senior leadership level roles for a large corporation. This governance committee structure is for a company with four regional operations (A–D) across its global footprint. Your organization may have a different leadership structure managing these same functions or you may have additional critical functions you want to include. Consider this a starting point for your committee. The initial task is to select the right leadership roles to support the team's charter and organization's mission as effectively as possible.

Governance Committee Team Charter

In Chapter 2 we reviewed the importance of a charter as an effective tool to document and show commitment across your organization. Below is an example of a governance committee team charter for your operational resilience process. This charter is for a company with a structure of four regional operations across its global footprint. You can modify the example team charter to the size and structure of your company. Include references to the team's purpose and scope, along with your expectations on time commitments.

Table 4.1 An example governance committee structure

Team	Name	Title	Role
Communications		Chief Communications Officer	The Chief Communications Officer or equivalent leads internal, external, and crisis communications.
Environment, Health, Safety and Sustainability		Environment, Health, Safety and Sustainability Officer	The most senior Environment, Health, Safety and Sustainability leader has responsibility for related compliance activities and organizational commitments.
Finance		Chief Financial Officer	The Chief Financial Officer or equivalent leads internal and external financial reporting, financial management of the organization's assets, and corporate cash management.
Human Resources		Chief Human Resource Officer	The Chief Human Resource Officer or equivalent develops and executes associate related strategies to support the overall business plan and strategic direction of the organization.
Information Technology		Chief Information Officer	The Chief Information Officer or equivalent manages, evaluates, and assesses how the organization is handling its information technology resources and leads the global information security program.
Legal		General Counsel	The General Counsel or equivalent is the organization's main attorney and primary source of legal advice integral to business decision making.

(Continued)

Table 4.1 (Continued)

Team	Name	Title	Role
Global Operations		Chief Operating Officer	The Chief Operating Officer or equivalent establishes global processes and improvements and ensures all department leaders are fully informed of and comply with global operational objectives.
Region A Operations		Region A Operations Leader	The regional operations leader establishes regional processes and process improvements for Region A and ensures all department leaders are fully informed of and comply with regional operational objectives.
Region B Operations		Region B Operations Leader	The regional operations leader establishes regional processes and process improvements for Region B and ensures all department leaders are fully informed of and comply with regional operational objectives.
Region C Operations		Region C Operations Leader	The regional operations leader establishes regional processes and process improvements for Region C and ensures all department leaders are fully informed of and comply with regional operational objectives.
Region D Operations		Region D Operations Leader	The regional operations leader establishes regional processes and process improvements for Region D and ensures all department leaders are fully informed of and comply with regional operational objectives.

(Continued)

Table 4.1 (Continued)

Team	Name	Title	Role
Procurement		Chief Procurement Officer	The Chief Procurement Officer or equivalent leads the organization's purchasing function and oversees the acquisition of goods and services to meet needs while helping to reduce costs and improve profits.
Quality		Chief Quality Officer	The most senior quality leader is responsible for monitoring the quality of products or services provided by the organization.
Business Continuity		Global Business Continuity Leader	The most senior business continuity leader manages the planning and implementation of an effective and well aligned organizational resilience process.

Governance Committee Charter Components

Purpose: Provide leadership and direction for a consistent and integrated approach in implementing a global operational resilience process including preparing for, responding to, and effectively recovering from crises and business continuity events.

Scope: Company owned or operated manufacturing and non-manufacturing facilities and related critical business processes.

Committee Members: Include the governance committee structure referenced in Table 4.1.

- Chief Communications Officer
- Environment, Health, Safety and Sustainability Officer
- Chief Financial Officer
- Chief Human Resource Officer
- Chief Information Officer
- General Counsel
- Chief Operating Officer
- Region A Operations Leader
- Region B Operations Leader
- Region C Operations Leader

- Region D Operations Leader
- Chief Procurement Officer
- Chief Quality Officer
- Global Business Continuity Leader

Meeting Agenda and Cadence: Quarterly meetings led by the global business continuity organization include the following:

- Quarterly review of operational resilience activities.
- Updates to global and regional objectives and performance metrics.
- Takeaways from crises and critical business continuity events.
- Sharing regional best practices to address business risks.
- Alignment on improvements to maintain resilience.

Global Business Continuity Team Structure

The global business continuity function plays a major role in managing some of the most impactful components of an effective operational resilience process. These components include structuring, communicating, and supporting policies; risk-based decision making; critical process identification; project planning; and prioritization of recovery activities. Additional resilience activities will be referenced in upcoming chapters. Among factors to consider when reflecting on the business continuity function are the following:

Reporting Structure

It's critical that you have the right reporting structure at the appropriate management level to empower effectiveness. Since we are targeting operational resilience, it is most beneficial to have the business continuity function report directly to the highest level of operational leadership. We've defined that role to be the Chief Operating Officer, or its equivalent. This reporting structure allows the business continuity function to have direct involvement and decision-making ability on operational risks, critical business processes, and strategies. Some organizations have established the role of Chief Resilience Officer. The Chief Resilience Officer has responsibility for interacting with senior executives and regulatory officials and speaks to the organization's overall resilience approach. Many of the functions with strategic responsibility for resilience will report directly to the Chief Resilience Officer.

Strategic thinking is necessary in developing long-term, broad goals in operational resilience. If the business continuity function reports to a lower level of leadership, it becomes more of a tactical function with less opportunity for strategic decision making.

Your reporting structure will likely be influenced by the executive who is driving operational resilience in your organization. This executive can be any of the governance committee members and is ideally the senior operational function leader. The organization's culture, compliance requirements, and departmental alignments all contribute to where the business continuity position resides.

Title

The appropriate title of the business continuity leader also plays a factor in the strategic impact of the role. Titles define positions in companies relative to others, including the internal perception of responsibility and accountability which may affect a leader's capability to be effective. External perceptions of the importance of the role are also affected by the title of the function in the organization. When the business continuity leader has a title with an elevated status, it makes external benchmarking with piers much easier and more meaningful. The same can be said for working with external suppliers and customers.

Supporting Roles

In addition to the primary global business continuity role, additional supporting roles are necessary to effectively execute the most critical objectives, goals, and measures. The number of team members will be influenced by the size of the organization and agreed upon blocks of work. Here are examples of global business continuity team roles and a few of their primary tasks in support of operational resilience.

Business Continuity Director

- Extensive interaction and experience in all aspects of the function.
- Develop global department's annual operating plan.
- Focus on long-term strategic planning.
- Align business strategies with most senior organizational executives.

Business Continuity Manager

- Facilitate and oversee day-to-day operations of the department.
- Ensure major tasks and projects are completed on time.
- Interface with relevant stakeholders.

Business Continuity Program Manager

- Oversee completion of larger organizational goals.
- Coordinate activities between multiple projects.

Business Continuity Analyst

- Assist business continuity department team on all activities.
- Maintain relevant documentation in support of annual planning.

See Figure 4.1 as an example of a suggested business continuity structure for a global organization that includes the governance committee, global, regional, tactical and facility teams we continue to reference. We will provide recommendations for team training, frequency of engagement, and additional resilience-based activities in upcoming chapters.

Regional Business Continuity Team Structure

The regional business continuity leader for each operating region can have similar responsibilities as the global leader. They can all have the same title and have similar responsibilities with accountability for activities across

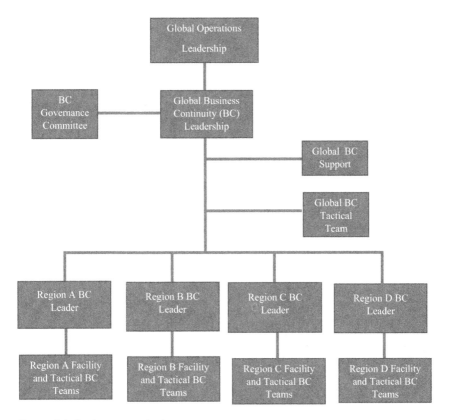

Figure 4.1 Business continuity team structure.

their respective region's operations. Like the global business continuity leader role, the reporting structure, title, and responsibilities show internal and external stakeholders the level of importance the organization places on the role. The regional leader should have a dotted line reporting structure to the global leader for input and feedback on common annual business continuity related objectives and performance metrics.

Tactical and Facility Operational Support

The term "tactical team" has been used in police and military-based organizations to define specialized units tasked with resolving high-level risks and critical incidents. They require specialized training, skills, and competencies to be successful during stressful events. Similarly, business continuity tactical team members are subject-matter experts in their organization. They use their training and expertise gained from daily responsibilities to support operational teams during incidents, crises, and business continuity events. Tactical team members focus on executing tasks based on their job function during high-risk situations requiring application of their specialized skills. By working with global and regional business continuity teams, the organization benefits from well-skilled teams that provide their expertise in resolving and benefiting from high-level risks and critical incidents. Global and regional business continuity leaders can select which departmental functions should have representatives and alternates on their tactical teams. Consider all roles that can support operational teams when responding to operational risks. See Table 4.2 for an example of tactical

Table 4.2 Tactical team members

Tactical Team	Principle Member Name	Alternate Member Name
Communications		
Environment, Health, Safety and Sustainability		
Finance		
Global Engineering		
Health and Medical		
HR		
IT		
Legal		
Logistics		
Procurement		
Quality		
Risk Management		
Security		
Supply Chain		

team members supporting a global organization. Each organization can modify their operational tactical support team membership structure as appropriate.

Tactical Team Responsibilities

Business continuity tactical team members should have clearly defined roles and team-based objectives. They should also receive annual training on what's expected of them and updates to training when appropriate in new activities.

Global and regional tactical teams can differ slightly but should remain aligned on how they support operational resilience. Below are suggested roles and activities to consider for both your global and regional business continuity tactical team members:

Communications team members manage the media and social media. They draft internal and external communications and assist with major incident notifications.

Environmental, Health, Safety and Sustainability team members primary focus is associate, contractor and visitor safety. They manage safety training, investigate safety-related incidents and report on environmental incidents. The facility Environment, Health, Safety and Sustainability team members work closely with global and regional teams. They also monitor and update job safety analyses and procedures.

Finance team members assist with out-of-process cost tracking. They act as a liaison with global risk management, treasury, and cash management.

Global Engineering team members assist with project management, including advising on reference documents such as drawings, specifications, and contracts. They work directly with critical equipment manufacturers and provide technical support with detailed damage assessments of facilities, utilities, and equipment.

Health and Medical team members act as liaison with local and external medical communities (e.g., hospitals, health departments, WHO, CDC, etc.). They manage grief counseling and overall infectious disease matters. They review and benchmark all matters related to health service.

Human Resources (HR) team members provide HR guidance to all associates regarding benefits, team development and succession planning before, during and after an incident. They manage the CBA process and direct associates with incident-related benefits to the correct benefit provider. They work with other teams to coordinate additional or temporary staffing for recovery efforts.

Information Technology (IT) team members keep critical IT systems and applications up and running. They maintain IT readiness at designated off-site locations, manage IT major incident notification, coordinate and prioritize IT issues with business process owners and advise on cyber security strategies.

Legal team members review internally and externally published documents along with reviewing contracts and agreements when needed. They provide general legal counsel for response and recovery.

Logistics team members coordinate shipment of materials (raw and finished products) throughout the entire process including ports, trucking, transportation, etc. They coordinate potential issues with customs, port strikes and stay up-to-date on regional programs and processes relating to logistics and transportation. All logistics centers are managed by them.

Procurement team members coordinate overall raw material sourcing which includes managing available volumes of critical raw materials, selection of critical suppliers and coordination of emergency purchases. They also assist with approval or restoration contractor activities and selection of alternate site locations.

Quality team members provide support in the evaluation of materials that may be out of the normal process mode by testing alternate materials to meet quality specifications prior to production. They coordinate closely with all other teams on the material risk evaluation process.

Risk Management team members coordinate with the insurance adjustor to assure prompt restoration and recovery activities. They document proof of losses, submit claims, monitor payments, and negotiate equivalencies with property insurers.

Security team members provide and maintain the emergency operations center for monitoring, alerting, and reporting on all security activities. They coordinate travel advisories, mass notification, and provide intelligence on all security matters.

Supply Chain team members coordinate overall sourcing and supply of raw materials and finished goods. This includes monitoring deviations to normal processes, modifying allocations for potential shortages and providing data linking key materials to finished goods for optimal prioritization.

Facility Operational Support

Regional business continuity leaders and tactical teams work directly with facilities that are part of their operational reporting structure. You can identify a single individual to manage all business continuity activities at the local facility level. Their reporting structure can include both the facility manager for all local activities and the regional business continuity leader for regional business continuity activities. Additional details on their operational objectives and specific activities tied to operational resilience are provided in subsequent chapters. For now, consider them as the main point of contact on all business continuity objectives and goals aligned with the regional business continuity function. In addition, remember to have alternates identified and trained for these and all other roles. Succession planning is a critical part of your operational resilience process.

Operational Incident Response

We've defined an incident as an event having the potential to cause interruption, disruption, loss, emergency, disaster, or catastrophe. Quite often, incidents occur at a facility that require a local response to support associates, protect the facility, or maintain business operations. The facility requires a clearly defined response plan that is compliant with local regulations and that is ready to be implemented by well-trained key personnel. The incident response team must be prepared to respond to both high- probability and high-impact local risks that can quickly escalate to major incidents and crises. The incident manager must be aware of how the team will interact with the regional business continuity team and crisis management team. The incident response may include an evacuation of the facility, sheltering in place, or any other measure needed to return the operations to pre-incident mode.

Business Continuity Event

A business continuity event occurs when an organization experiences an incident that impacts critical business processes such as its ability to manufacture or deliver products and services at an acceptable predetermined level. The business continuity plan should be prepared in advance for high-probability, high-impact, and novel risks that may affect facility or business operations. Procedures and information that have been developed and maintained by the appropriate business continuity team are included in the response. The team's goal is to implement viable recovery strategies and maintain continuity of services. We will cover how facility incident response, business continuity, and crisis management teams work together later in this chapter. First, let's review how business continuity teams engage in support of the organization through different stages of the event.

A Business Continuity Event is Initiated

1. Determine who should attend the initial business continuity meeting based on the scope of the event (e.g., local or regional support team members, facility affected, etc.).
2. Schedule and conduct an overview of the event with those attending the meeting.
3. Determine the type and scale of impact to associates, the facility, and business operations.
4. Provide the event summary to those who attended the meeting and anyone who will attend any follow-up meetings.
5. Schedule the next meeting and include any additional support team members needed.
6. Determine the tools needed to support the entire team throughout the event, including business continuity software, response plans, action lists, etc.
7. Prepare a distribution list for meeting summaries.

Extended Business Continuity Engagement is Underway

1. Conduct the follow-up meeting covering:

   - The latest status update and its impact on the facility or region.
   - The appropriate workstreams (e.g., tactical or support functions such as communications, HR, manufacturing, risk management, etc.) for future meetings.
   - All available courses of action to support associates, minimize cost impact, and speed up the recovery process.
   - Any long-term corrective measures that are immediately identified.
   - The name of each workstream leader who will manage appropriate actions.
   - A determination as to whether out-of-process cost tracking is required.

2. Prior to closure of each meeting, recap the following:

   - Action items (primary team tasks) from that meeting.
   - Workstream leaders who will report on each action item in the next meeting.
   - Deadlines or anticipated completion dates for each item.
   - Status of the event that will determine return to normal operations (pre-business continuity event mode).
   - Cadence for follow up meetings (daily, weekly, etc.).

3. Complete and distribute the meeting summary.
4. Schedule future meetings.

5. Manage future meetings as referenced above, including a recap of action items status and any new activities.
6. Notify the regional crisis management team of the severity of the team's engagement and align with the crisis management team leader on the appropriate course of action.

A Business Continuity Event is Coming to a Close

Once the event is coming to a close:

- Develop appropriate survey questions for lessons learned/process improvement.
- Distribute the survey to the appropriate team members, along with a due date for completion.
- Review responses from the survey.
- Complete a summary of the responses and distribute it to the interested audience.
- Conduct a meeting on lessons learned from the event.
- Distribute the lessons learned summary to event participants for feedback.
- Gather responses from survey participants.
- Consolidate feedback from the team by workstream.
- Identify gaps in planning that were evident during the event or response.

Post-Event Gap Analysis is Underway

Once the event is resolved and the business continuity engagement has concluded:
- Distribute the lessons learned to all other regional business continuity to share with their regional operations.
- Implement appropriate changes from the gap analysis, including documented plans and procedures.
- Monitor the effectiveness of updated plans and course of action during the next incident.
- Make appropriate changes as needed as part of continuous improvement.

Crisis Management Team

Having a well-trained and experienced crisis management team is a big contributor to remaining operationally resilient. A crisis necessitates a well-coordinated response to preserve life safety and physical infrastructure while minimizing operational impact. The crisis may initially affect any part or level of the organization and can escalate quickly. Therefore, it is essential that the organization has the right representatives on the crisis management team to take swift action in providing needed support. The team consists of senior operational decision makers trained in working with both incident response and business continuity teams. The crisis management team should know how to manage interactions between their team and others.

Table 4.3 provides a review of the suggested crisis management team. As with the governance committee this is for a global organization with four operational regions. The table includes the specific functions represented, their roles on the crisis management team, and a "RACI"[2] (Responsible, Accountable, Consulted, or Informed) matrix of how they

Table 4.3 Crisis management team RACI matrix

Crisis Management Team Roles and Responsibilities

Activity	CMT Leader	Operations	HR	Security	Communications	IT	Finance	Business Leader	Legal	Business Continuity
Main contact for crisis management team to escalate crisis related issues and engage the team	A	I	I	I	I	I	I	I	I	C
Participate in all crises in person or with an alternate	A	R	R	R	R	R	R	R	R	I
Maintain contact with crisis management team leader to engage business continuity team	R	C	C	C	C	C	C	C	C	A
Represent and engage all operational functions	C	A	C	C	C	C	C	C	C	I
Advise on associate activities	C	C	A	C	C	C	C	C	C	I
Advise on security activities	C	C	C	A	C	C	C	C	C	I
Advise on communication activities	C	C	C	C	A	C	C	C	C	I
Advise on all IT activities	C	C	C	C	C	A	C	C	C	I
Advise on finance activities	C	C	C	C	C	C	A	C	C	I
Advise on business activities	C	C	C	C	C	C	C	A	C	I
Advise on legal activities	C	C	C	C	C	C	C	C	A	I
Engage functional resources	A	R	R	R	R	R	R	R	R	I
Participate in post-incident reviews and lessons learned	A	R	R	R	R	R	R	R	R	C
Maintain current crisis management team documentation	A	C	C	C	C	C	C	C	C	C

interact within the team. A RACI matrix can be considered an assignment chart that has every task or key decision identified in order for the team to be successful.

Crisis Management Team Representatives

Crisis Management Team Leader: Main global and regional point of contact for the crisis management team who determines the need to escalate the event to a crisis level.

Operations: Represent and engage all operational functions.

Human Resources (HR): Advise on all activities related to associates.

Security: Advise on all security activities during crises.

Communications: Advise on all internal and external communication strategies.

Information Technology (IT): Advise on all IT matters (e.g., infrastructure, security, etc.).

Finance: Advise on all finance matters.

Business Leader: Advise on business unit matters.

Legal: Advise on legal matters.

Business Continuity: Maintain ongoing contact with the crisis management team leader to engage appropriate business continuity functions to support appropriate critical business processes.

Cross Functional Coordination

Recent crises like infectious disease outbreaks, facility shutdowns, and ransomware events can expose issues with team engagement and management throughout your organization. This could be caused by high turnover in roles and responsibilities in all functions, including those that support operational resilience. Another reason might be that one team may handle more than its share of responsibilities and others defer to them for all decision making. You'll benefit by having a well-defined method of awareness and training regarding the management of incidents, business continuity events, and crises. Your roadmap should include clarification on what crises are, what they are not, and how facility and regional teams can optimize their time. This helps promote seamless management of incidents, crises, and business continuity events both separately and collectively.

Team Planning

Let's review what incident response, crisis management, and business continuity teams should focus on in the planning stage. We will add a few figures you can reference to help with awareness and training for your operational teams.

Aligning on how escalation and transition can be most effective

Managing an incident, crisis, and a business continuity event are different activities that present different challenges to different teams. Incident management involves the immediate combination of facilities, equipment, personnel, procedures, and communications operating within a common organizational structure. A group of individuals are responsible for developing and implementing a comprehensive plan for responding to a disruptive incident. The team consists of a core group of decision makers trained in incident management and who are prepared to respond to any situation. Crisis management should focus on addressing reputational, financial, commercial, and strategic risks that expose the long-term viability of the company and could have been triggered from an operational incident. Business continuity events should focus on restoring critical business processes, so they do not adversely affect the organization's objectives and goals. Many of the companies I've benchmarked have a lack of clarity and alignment in how they transition between these three operational functions. This causes difficulties and challenges in making the best use of resources and in reaching the objective of returning to normal business operations.

The following actions will help to make your teams aware of how to differentiate between and manage incidents, crises, and business continuity events.

- Clearly identify the type and severity of the situation to determine if it has escalated from an incident to a crisis or business continuity event.
- Clarify roles of the teams, including documented plans that leave no doubt as to where responsibilities and accountability resides for each respective team.
- Define differences and separation between each function, shifting the focus between teams as needed so each team stays in their own lane.
- Monitor the team's activities and continue to remind team members when the overlap starts to shift the focus of their roles.
- Provide regular situation reports with action items underway in clear and nontechnical terms.
- Identify coordinators between the three groups to ensure they are operating effectively by addressing issues with coordination, maintaining separation between the teams, and providing consistency in strategic direction.
- Conduct training and exercises to develop individual and team "muscle memory" on how to work both together and separately.

- Establish a process with critical team members and alternates who are ready to engage. Include succession planning for all critical roles to avoid issues on team engagement and effectiveness.
- The goal is for every team to realize that a facility-related incident can quickly escalate to a crisis without business continuity involvement. A business continuity event may involve one or more facilities and not become a crisis. A crisis may include incident response and business continuity team engagement.

Team structure promoting efficient engagement

Let's recap how efficient operational decision making can occur from the facility level to executive leadership levels throughout your organization. We add executive leadership as first of the four teams in our analysis below and include the cross-functional teams in Figure 4.2.

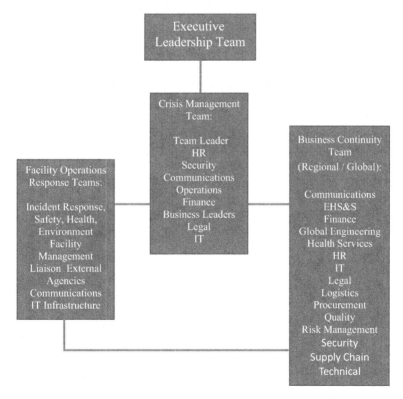

Figure 4.2 Cross-functional teams.

- **Executive Leadership Teams** maintain focus on the intent of the organization. They must affirm and refine organizational priorities when needed. Their role includes making strategic decisions and addressing escalated issues that may change the direction of the organization.
- **Crisis Management Teams** maintain centralized decision making for command and control. They help facilitate planning and guidance at a strategic level to help create conditions for effective operational execution.
- **Business Continuity Teams** manage regional and global engagement with overall critical process alignment. They identify, analyze, and manage workstreams to optimize overall response.
- **Incident Response Teams** handle immediate responses to risks and events. They are often the first team to assemble and respond due to their proximity to the incident.

Organizational Crisis Planning Roles and Responsibilities

Let's identify key activities between the four teams in planning for crises.

- Establish the overall framework, guidance, templates, and tools to support an effective crisis readiness and response capability.
- Define the action triggers, thresholds, and associated processes to assess and assign the severity level of a crisis or potential crisis.
- Plan for and acquire resources to establish and maintain the crisis management program.
- Develop (and update on a regular basis) crisis management priorities and a strategic roadmap.
- Develop and report on program metrics.
- Regularly evaluate the program to identify gaps and implement best practices.
- Maintain technology and tools for accurate program information.
- Develop the crisis management plans, playbooks, and supporting processes.
- Develop and update crisis plans and playbooks for all sites.

Team Execution

Let's review roles and responsibilities for effective team execution of duties during incidents, crises, and business continuity events. We will show how they can be mutually inclusive or exclusive.

Here are key activities between the four teams during the execution of crises.

- Plan and provide guidance on site-based incident response activities.
- Execute site-based incident response activities.
- Escalate issues or concerns to the crisis management team.
- Provide regional management and oversight as needed.
- Develop an operational cadence to guide overall response activities.
- Facilitate planning and develop recommended guidance and approaches.
- Acquire and allocate resources needed to support the crisis response.
- Use appropriate technology and tools to facilitate crisis response activities.
- Provide local or regional insights and expertise as needed.
- Provide global management if the incident escalates requiring a greater level of support.
- Plan and provide guidance on the execution of site-based response activities.
- Provide guidance throughout the incident, crisis, and business continuity event until it is resolved.
- Facilitate a post-incident review to identify best practices, lessons learned, and potential gaps.
- Formally declare end of the "crisis" and return to normal operations.

Mutually inclusive or exclusive activities

Responses to incidents, crises and business continuity events can be mutually inclusive or mutually exclusive.

- A facility related incident can quickly escalate to a crisis without business continuity team involvement (exclusive)
- A business continuity even may involve one or more facilities and not become a crisis (inclusive)
- A crisis may include incident response and business continuity team engagement (inclusive)

Continuous Improvement

To continuously improve means to steadily improve over time. To be resilient means to adapt to difficult experiences with flexibility. As your teams execute actions in response to incidents, crises, and business continuity events, resilience requires a continuous improvement mindset. I've had quite a bit of success in getting cross-functional teams to provide valuable suggestions on improvements needed. Consider taking the following actions as soon as you become aware of issues while these activities are still underway.

Monitor activities and workstreams as they are occurring. If anything must change while your response is underway, do it immediately. If something isn't exactly as you like, make note of it and include it in what you are tracking to improve the team's work in the future. Either way, continue to track all activities you believe need improvement for more effective team engagement. Continue to follow this method of improving each workstream until you return to normal operations.

Survey the team participants once an event has concluded. Consider sending the survey to everyone who has somehow participated in the event. An example of survey questions is included below. You will most likely get a response to surveys that are brief, that reference activities that the team is familiar with, and that are written in a positive, not negative tone.

Crisis Management Supply Chain Response Survey

1) Was our crisis management process effectively implemented?
   a) Yes.
   b) No.
   c) Please provide further comments here.

2) Were the right individuals involved throughout our team's response?
   a) Yes.
   b) No.
   c) Please provide further comments here.

3) Was enough focus given to all team categories throughout our team's response?
   a) Yes.
   b) No.
   c) Please provide further comments here.

4) Did internal teams accurately implement business continuity plans throughout the response and recovery?
   a) Yes.
   b) No.
   c) Please provide further comments here.

5) Did external teams accurately implement business continuity plans throughout the response and recovery?
   a) Yes.
   b) No.
   c) Please provide further comments here.

6) Please provide comments on which strategies worked well and which need improvement.

7) Please provide suggestions that will benefit us during future operational crises.

Summarize the survey results by workstream. Include all comments. You may receive a significant number of comments on a single workstream indicating an obvious need for improvement. Other workstreams may receive very positive survey comments if an individual or entire team is executing very effectively. Regardless, include every comment received in your summary.

Share the consolidated results with all participants. Doing so sends the message that you value their feedback and are focused on continuous improvement. This promotes a team concept and will likely keep everyone better engaged in the future. Also share the results of the survey with all other operational regions so they can benefit from the team's feedback. Include the number of team members who received the survey and how many responded. Some believe that a response rate of over 25 percent is an indicator of success. Regardless of the number of responses, a single response with a meaningful comment can provide significant positive impact.

Track progress on actionable items until they are implemented. This can be done quite simply. Develop a spreadsheet that includes SMART objectives tied to the team's feedback.

Update applicable plans, playbooks, and documents to benefit teams in similar future events. If it is a significant recommendation, update plans immediately. If not, update the documents during the next calendar cycle as appropriate.

Test revised plans through exercises and proactive discussions. As referenced throughout my book, tabletop exercises are a great way to build team confidence for managing high probability and high impact risks. The exercises should have an end goal in mind, such as validating actions recommended because of a major crisis or event. I've found brief exercises merged into other reoccurring meetings to be incredibly beneficial. You can reach a large audience without creating a new meeting and affecting their blocks of work. Being time conscious is appreciated by everyone attending the exercise.

Validate corrective action is in place in future events. Monitor the team's response and actions during similar future events. This validates the accuracy of recommendations from the previous event and helps promote process improvement.

Repeat this same process in all future major events. Your teams know they are part of an operationally resilient mindset that values their input. Following similar actions during every crisis or event builds the team's capabilities and expectations for future success.

Dynamic Execution

Use a dynamic approach in leading, following, and guiding, constantly adapting to the current events in which you're involved. Regardless of all the work that goes into planning and building operational resilience, how your teams execute when needed is what everyone remembers. It's what is most visible to your teams, your associates, leadership, and the public. Were we successful or did we fail? Our goal is to build team capabilities so that every response has minimal issues, is effective, and attains success. Having alternates identified and trained in critical roles betters your odds of success. Providing the right support for your teams in training and in executions is also a critical factor for success. We've defined teams that are integral to success in operational resilience. We continue to highlight behaviors that benefit us throughout our journey. Effective leadership includes having a flexible approach to supporting both your associates and business goals. An ongoing engagement with all stakeholders allows you to meet objectives the right way. Having a focus on empathy, communication, and being flexible to balance needs with goals is what we focus on.

Now let's review some suggestions on ensuring your teams stay consistently engaged and execute dynamically.

Align your entire network of teams

Ensure that every team is aware of the others' existence, their structures, roles, responsibilities, and how they tie together in a common vision. Include how they should execute handoffs between teams. Provide training on these networking concepts. Continue to build the knowledge base for a well-unified team.

Launch your teams quickly

Engaging your teams quickly is a priority. Ensure your teams are structured right and always ready. Notify them as soon as an issue escalates and keep them updated on the current status. They need to be flexible and ready to respond to the latest information. Correct their course of action if needed as they move forward.

Stay engaged but allow your teams to do their work

Make sure they are aware of who is leading which workstream and when your next touch point will be. Keep open dialogue between each workstream leader in case issues come up prior to the next scheduled touch point. Stay connected but stay out of their way. You've trusted them so far. Place trust in them to execute well.

Maintain transparency to help promote clear and accurate communication

Actions should be taken based on current facts. Sharing the latest facts helps promote appropriate risk-based decision making and effective team collaboration. Everyone knows there will be uncertainty during challenging events. A transparent culture ensures all teams are aligned on the right actions being taken and that corrections are expected and will be appropriately addressed without punishing anyone. You want to hear and need to hear when things aren't going as expected so that you can quickly take corrective action. Provide psychological support so that individuals and teams can quickly share information, make the changes needed, and learn from unexpected issues.

Allow self-managing so all teams can be most effective

As the sizes of teams increase, it's more difficult for all team members to relate to each other all the time. They need to know how to work within their teams and with other teams. Workstream or operational leaders should have the latitude to make decisions for their teams without interference from any other team or group. This allows all teams to move forward quickly and effectively. Keeping the right work environment during challenging times makes your teams feel appreciated, encourages them to give it their best, and lets them to know the organization truly appreciates all that they do.

Communicate consistently and effectively

One of the greatest challenges during any event, including a crisis, is accurate and effective communication. You can overcome this challenge by explaining exactly what's needed, including when and why. Communicate clearly, simply, and often so that issues that could escalate can be promptly addressed and eliminated. Use every tool you have to your advantage. Remember you may have teams with multiple backgrounds, languages, and cultures. Repeating important points provides clarity and removes ambiguity which goes a long way to avoid misunderstandings. Provide for inclusivity by encouraging mass participation in teams to get better results. Listening more and mastering the art of asking the right questions is the best way to understand and appreciate the needs of your teams.

Overcoming your teams' fears is another issue you need to address. A slight element of fear always exists when responding to crises. Concerns include financial issues and the potential impact an event will have on your associates' families and their communities. A leader should be aware of which of these fears are present so they can provide the right support needed.

Be a considerate leader

Your team members look to you for guidance and support, so stay focused on that and set the right example. Keep them inspired, appreciated, and feeling rewarded for what they do. Don't forget to celebrate team successes with them. No matter how challenging things are, if you remain committed and energized, your team will follow suit. Don't use controlling language or provide unrealistic deadlines that cannot be met. Keep in mind that a leader leads by also being a team member, not everyone else's superior. Knowing the roles and responsibilities of each team member is quite important. Ask questions in a way that allows each team member to provide their expertise to promote team engagement. Show empathy, trust, support and care for your teams.

Maintain your team's wellbeing

Your team likely consists of many individuals who excel in their functional roles. They are likely expected to drop everything and support your operations during very challenging events and crises. This can be very demanding on their personal, team, and family schedules. Prioritizing their safety, health, and mental wellbeing will help keep them healthy, happy, and motivated. Remind them you care about them and not just their productivity. Get leadership support for well trained and committed alternates in critical roles so everyone can take a break as needed to decompress and refresh.

Most organizations state their associates are their number one asset. Your actions will help clarify if that statement is actually accurate. As stated above, remember to celebrate the team's successes by recognizing and celebrating accomplishments of significance during challenging times. This plays a huge role in building morale, a sense of belonging, and cohesiveness. Your words have power and impact. Gratitude is a powerful way to reinforce team culture and build resilience.

How to Lead, Follow and Guide the Way

Teams that are well structured perform, communicate, and function as a cohesive unit and can meet or exceed any objective they undertake. The following team-based concepts are an essential part of operational resilience.

o **Structure your teams to be operationally aligned throughout your organization.** Your resilience-based teams should be aligned with your operational functions. Your corporate website is a good reference to follow. Your governance committee should include top operational leaders with a clearly defined charter. Business continuity teams at both the global and regional level provide important leadership throughout the resilience journey. Tactical and facility-based operational team members have expertise that is of value during high-risk situations.

o **Prepare your teams for optimal execution during incidents, crises, and business continuity events.** Have a common understanding of who will manage incidents, crises, and business continuity events. Include how teams will interact to maximize their value to your associates and to the business. Conduct the right training so they are ready for your top operational risks.

o **Improve your team's performance through gap analysis and process improvement.** Track any issues that appear while your teams are engaged. Survey your teams as the event is coming to a close. Summarize the survey results including gaps and provide process improvement suggestions. Share the results with the participants and others who will benefit by the improvement recommendations.

o **Build team capability to execute dynamically.** Engage your teams as soon as their expertise is needed. Allow them to do what they do best while staying close by and providing support when needed. Share the good news, bad news, and relevant information as soon as it's available. Keep them inspired, appreciated, and feeling rewarded for what they do. Don't forget to celebrate team successes. Prioritize their safety, health, and mental wellbeing.

How to Lead

Analyze your present organizational structure and any imminent business-related changes so that your teams are structured for the long term. Update the documents in your toolbox to suit the teams you are structuring. Include an overview of your method of managing incidents, crises, and business continuity events. Prepare an easy-to-use method for surveying your teams and getting feedback on what worked well and what did not. Be aware of dynamic execution techniques to get the best out of your teams.

How to Follow

Stay closely aligned with your executive sponsor and governance committee members. Obtain necessary approvals prior to moving forward. Make necessary changes to team structure, training, and overall engagement.

How to Guide the Way

Move forward with a team-based approach that promotes operational resilience. You have structured the teams well, so allow them to manage what's expected of them. Communicate regularly and effectively with simple instructions that can be easily understood and followed during complex situations. Watch how your teams manage the handoffs between one another and provide feedback where needed. Allow each team member to use their skill to benefit your operations. Maintain team motivation by prioritizing their safety, health, and mental wellbeing. Celebrate successes and be transparent when issues arise. Stay focused on a common approach across all global and regional operations. Continue to modify your roadmap and remain focused on continuous improvement.

Notes

1 https://your.yale.edu/we-know-teamwork-important-how-important
2 Dana Miranda and Rob Watts, 'What Is A RACI Chart? How This Project Management Tool Can Boost Your Productivity', Forbes Advisor, https://www.forbes.com/advisor/business/raci-chart/

Chapter V

Resilient Deployment

The next step in your operational resilience journey is executing the strategic activities for which you've built support. We'll call this resilient deployment. You're using tools from your toolbox, engaging your teams, and executing strategies to achieve your goals. Having a common focus on objectives and activities that are aligned with the organization's strategy is an integral part of resilient deployment. You need to know how each objective supports the strategy and how the teams' daily actions accurately relate to the strategy. We've reviewed how your project plan's short- and long-term goals and objectives are a part of your journey. The timing of when and how you use your tools are also essential elements of resilient deployment. Place your focus on clearly understanding, supporting, and defining steps to support the organization's strategy. The concept of continuous improvement (Plan, Do, Check, Act) should be followed to ensure that as objectives are established, the right actions are taken, validated, and modified as necessary. Actions you're taking on a global scale need to also include all business regions. Your main goal should be consistently applying strategies, sharing progress toward them on a frequent basis, and modifying plans to stay in alignment with the organization's mission.

In this chapter we will provide a comprehensive review of the following concepts to assist you in the identification, execution, and improvement of resilient deployment strategies:

- Documented Project Plan
- Aligned Business Objectives
- Scorecard Reporting
- Risks Assessed
- Critical Processes Identified
- Impact Tolerance
- Business Continuity Plans, Playbooks, and Documentation
- Maintaining Progress

DOI: 10.4324/9781003438700-5

We'll also review why some companies succeed and others fail in executing their intended strategies.

Documented Project Plan

We identified project planning as one of the first and most important activities in a well-defined roadmap of how your teams' work supports the organization's resilience. By having an agreed-upon project schedule, you have a clear understanding of how every item ties back to the organization's mission and goals. As referenced earlier, consider using a mix of cloud-based applications, software, spreadsheets, and documents to help simplify the execution of your plan and provide clarity across your organization. The tools you select and use can be the primary method of tracking your team's progress per the project plan.

Let's create a project plan that includes the concepts we've covered which you can easily apply to your organization. The examples are based on a global organization with four regional business units and teams we've previously defined. See Figure 5.1 for components of a documented project plan.

Long-Term Planning (three to five years)

We begin by identifying a purpose statement to clarify our focus and communicate goals to all our team members. No matter what role a team

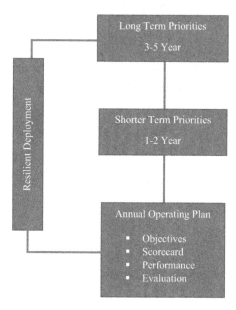

Figure 5.1 Documented project plan.

member has, the purpose statement provides focus and alignment on reaching relevant goals. Next, we include long-term strategic goals to help us focus on the team's purpose. A three to five-year plan can significantly increase the likelihood you will achieve goals by giving you the ability to adjust short-term steps as you focus on the long term.

An example of a purpose statement is: Be the Most Resilient Global Manufacturer.

"Best in Class" is a term commonly used to identify a product or something else that is the best of its kind. It means you're better than your competition. To achieve this status, you must be a top performer, and per our definition, you must be resilient.

Examples of three to five-year strategic goals:

- Implement a Best in Class operationally resilient process across all global regions in the next three years.
- All global regions conduct onsite strategic audits of their programs in the next three years.
- All global regions have fully certified business continuity leaders in full-time equivalent roles.
- Tactical business support functions conduct resilience-based audits with their primary, secondary, and third tier suppliers.

Shorter-Term Priorities (one to two years)

Let's include key mid-term objectives to be completed within a two-year time span. Tie your objectives back to your long-term planning and allow for adjustments to your three-year goals in the short term.

Example of one to two-year strategic goals:

- Implement process improvement of your objectives from an established baseline to attain Best in Class resilience goals.
- Develop a method to conduct strategic internal audits across all global regions.
- Begin to implement training and attain certification qualifications for all business continuity leaders.
- Coordinate execution of the upcoming global supplier audit program.

Immediate Priorities (current year)

Finally, we add immediate strategic priorities for the upcoming year that are the basis for annual objectives across all business units. This can be done with an Annual Operating Plan (AOP). Let's define the team's AOP to include the key objectives, goals, and measures to achieve your annual priorities. The AOP ties directly to your long-term planning and helps to identify day-to-day frameworks and resources required to reach agreed-upon results.

Example of current-year objectives:

- Define the baseline to attain Best in Class resilience goals.
- Develop onsite strategic audit components for all global regions.
- Obtain leadership support and funding for the regional certification process of all business continuity leaders.
- Develop a globally aligned supplier audit program.

Aligned Business Objectives

Current-year objectives are closely tied to your immediate priorities and remain a part of the long-term plan supporting the organization's purpose. We'll review individual team members' objectives that tie back to these business objectives in the next chapter. As you're developing these objectives, consider conducting a SWOT analysis as previously described. Here is a recap of the SWOT analysis that we will sync up with the current-year objectives.

Internal Strengths and Weaknesses

Evaluate some of the activities that support effective operational resilience across your organization and determine whether there are visible strengths or weaknesses that tie to them. Below are some of the activities that may apply based on our model organization and what we've covered so far. Determine if they are presently a strength, or a weakness needing process improvement in your organization.

- Has your organization developed a resilience-based policy?
- Do you already have a process to identify and manage risks?
- Are all facilities aligned in a common way to report major incidents?
- Do your facilities manage incidents effectively?
- Are all the global regions aligned in a common business continuity process?
- Do you have a continuous improvement culture and process in place?
- Is resilience seen as a primary or secondary priority?
- Have you identified critical business processes?
- Do you have planning in place to quickly recover business processes?

External Opportunities and Threats

Include external factors you've noted in your resilience journey to date. Determine if they are presently a strength or a weakness needing process improvement. Consider some of the following items as either external opportunities or threats:

- Do similar industries, your competition, and critical suppliers value operational resilience?
- Are there defined customer expectations for continuity of operations?
- Are there investor relations and market expectations regarding operational resilience?
- Are there IT based risks currently impacting your operations (e.g., cyber security, ransomware, etc.)?
- Are there geopolitical risks affecting your associates and business operations?
- Have you experienced evolving government requirements regarding continuity of operations?
- Have human, facility, and infrastructural issues affected raw materials and finished goods production and delivery to customers?

Current-Year Objectives

We've reviewed how current-year objectives are immediate priorities that tie back to your long-term planning. Keep current-year objectives simple and SMART to make them more easily understood and less ambiguous. Think about how your internal and external strengths and weaknesses play a role in supporting them. Let's review examples of the objectives that tie to our project planning in the current year below.

- Align all teams on common objectives by the end of first quarter of the year.
- Create regional alignment on blocks of work to attain current-year objectives by January 31 and track progress monthly throughout the year.
- Incorporate resilience training with all team members by the end of the first quarter of the year.
- Implement a resilience-based scorecard in line with current-year goals by January 31 and track progress toward attaining goals monthly throughout the year.
- Test and validate resilience plans through tabletop exercises in all facilities by the end of the second quarter of the year.
- Develop a process to track business continuity maturity and identify objectives for the following year by the end of the third quarter of the year.

Scorecard Reporting

Next, let us develop a scorecard that includes a combination of qualitative and quantitative data. Our goal is to improve the evaluation of our results by ensuring the limitations of one type of data are balanced by the strength of the other type. Both types of data include relevant items that tie back to our project planning and regionally aligned objectives throughout the year. We will include an example of how to track overall progress of both types monthly. The items on our scorecard are the KPIs referenced in Chapter 2. They give organizations a better way to understand the progress regional and global teams make on key business goals both monthly and annually. Consider the example below which rates both quantitative and qualitative scorecard components equally. It's a great way to track your progress on activities that support operational resilience.

Quantitative Scorecard Components

We will reference scorecard data that includes calendar-based activities to help support your resilience journey. Below are a few suggested activities with a reasonable attainment timeframe that can be shared with appropriate operational team members. Upcoming chapters in this book will include details regarding the scorecard activities referenced below.

Monthly reporting can include the following four items, equally rated at 25 percent of your total score:

1) AOP on target.
2) Blocks of work being maintained.
3) Regional supporting roles confirmed.
4) Alignment with all facility-based teams.

Quarterly reporting can include the percentage of required regional team members attending and participating in meetings focused on operational resilience.

Additional **calendar-based** documents and activities can include completion of risk assessments; business impact analyses; business continuity plans, playbooks, and one-pagers; tabletop exercises; crisis management team training; and maturity model surveys. Further details on these documents and activities are provided throughout this book.

The monthly score can include the percentage of regional team members completing the tasks on time by region.

The quantitative activities above will amount to 50 percent of the scorecard results.

Qualitative Scorecard Components

A qualitative scorecard measures the quality of results, rather than the quantity of items completed per a defined calendar schedule. Let's include two activities that help validate the work supporting resilience is effective, is understood, and is adding business value in your organization.

Internal audit: This can provide excellent support in validating whether project planning objectives and goals are being executed by your teams as expected. The goal is to have evidence that each facility is compliant with regional and global expectations. When no internal audit findings are identified, you are 100 percent compliant with your intended objectives. We will provide suggestions on how to set up the internal audit site support process in upcoming chapters.

Effective management of incidents, crises, and business continuity events: Factors to consider in this KPI include:

1) Business downtime was less than or equal to the time expected or better than the defined time to recover business processes.
2) The business continuity plan, playbook, or one-pager was effectively used to the benefit of the team.
3) Communication was effective and occurred as the region expected.
4) Every team expected to participate across the region was engaged.
5) Corrective actions were developed and shared with appropriate team members.

The results of these five factors will be equally weighted at 20 percent each in the combined monthly score for effective qualitative results.

The qualitative activities will amount to the remaining 50 percent of the scorecard results.

Combined Monthly Scorecard

The combined monthly scorecard in Table 5.1 should be shared with global and regional operational leadership and other interested stakeholders. The monthly results show progress on aligned activities supporting current-year objectives. Your monthly scorecard should include an explanation of anything major that caused negative scorecard results the previous month. This is a great opportunity to create visibility for the team's successes and challenges in meeting objectives. Maintain a monthly cadence of reporting on what matters the most through the scorecard. It allows you to make changes as needed to remain aligned on your annual activities and targets. Your combined monthly scorecard can provide equal weighting to both quantitative and qualitative results to highlight their equal importance.

Table 5.1 Combined scorecard

Monthly Scorecard Results

Regional Summary KPI Score = Percent of All Regional Facilities Completing Activities on Time	Monthly AOP on Target	Risk Assessments Completed	Business Impact Analysis Completed	Business Continuity Plans and Playbooks Completed	Quarterly Regional Meetings Completed	Annual Team Training Completed	Tabletop Exercises Completed	Maturity Survey Completed	Audit Finding Results	Business Continuity Events and Crises Managed	Monthly KPI Score
Region A											
Region B											
Region C											
Region D											
Global Average											

Risks Assessed

We dedicated a chapter of this book to the benefits of turning risks into opportunities, the value of enterprise risk management, and the importance of having a common risk register across the organization. Now let's review how you can assess potential risks, accurately track actual incidents, and come up with the top operational risks across your organization. As referenced earlier, there are many ways you can gather data from your teams to prioritize risks that can impact your operations. They range from using a simple spreadsheet to utilizing a variety of software tools with improved user interface capabilities. Numerous risk assessment software tools are available depending on the type of business, revenue, size of organization, and sector. Methods of gathering risk-related information, analyzing data, and presenting results have become simpler.

Ready.gov[1] is an official website of the U.S. Department of Homeland Security. Ready Business is a section of their website dedicated to helping companies and businesses prepare for events, respond to them, and recover effectively. We'll reference examples from the ready.gov risk assessment site[2] along with generally accepted practices regarding assessing risk below. This will help you develop your own risk assessment template or provide insight into what to look for when obtaining a software license to implement a web or cloud-based risk assessment tool.

Ready Business Risk Assessment Table

Consider including the following steps taken from Ready Business[3] when developing your risk assessment process. Ready Business can be found through the ready.gov website. Included on their site is a risk assessment table. Their example is scalable, so you can add additional components that you want to track. It is a great starting point if you are new to the risk assessment process.

- Compile a list of assets (e.g., people, facilities, machinery, equipment, raw materials, finished goods, information technology, etc.)
- For each asset, list hazards that could cause an impact. Since multiple hazards could impact each asset, you will probably need to include them all for each asset. You can group assets together as necessary but highlight those assets that are highly valued or critical.
- For each hazard, consider both high probability/low impact scenarios and low probability/high impact scenarios.
- As you assess potential impacts, identify any vulnerabilities or weaknesses in the asset that would make it susceptible to loss. These vulnerabilities are opportunities for hazard prevention or risk mitigation.
- Record opportunities for prevention and mitigation.
- Estimate the probability that the scenarios will occur on a scale of "L" for low, "M" for medium, and "H" for high. Analyze the potential impact of the hazard scenario. Rate impacts "L" for low, "M" for medium, and "H" for high.
- Additional information regarding the Business Impact Analysis (BIA) can be referenced on the risk assessment table to rate the impact on "Operations."
- An "entity" column is referenced to estimate potential financial, regulatory, contractual, and brand/image/reputation impacts.
- The "Overall Hazard Rating" includes the "probability of occurrence" and the highest rating in impacts on people, property, operations, environment, and entity.
- Carefully review scenarios with potential impacts rated as "moderate" or "high."
- Consider whether action can be taken to prevent the scenario or to reduce the potential impacts.

Risks Included in Your Assessment Survey

Below are suggested human, natural, and technological risk assessment "hazards" to reference in the Ready Business Risk Assessment Table. In addition to production delays, for each hazard, consider potential impacts that have occurred within the previous two years.

- **Loss of staff and high absentee rates** – Gaps in filling important business roles, remote work concerns.
- **Work stoppage or strike potential** – Negative media publicity.
- **Civil unrest, riot, political and social instability** – Evacuations caused by bomb threats or other safety concerns, business interruptions due to protests or other events, inability to access facilities.
- **Crime and site security** – Facility theft and damage.
- **Product issues** – Product recalls, quality concerns.
- **Sabotage** – Damage to resources, products, and equipment.
- **Workplace violence or terrorism** – Verbal abuse or physical assaults.
- **Financial, economic, and inflation issues** – Reduced purchasing power, erosion of real income.
- **Ineffective method of mass notification** – Inability to manage the system and to contact associates.
- **Environmental incident** – Violations or fines, conditions that may require remediation.
- **Fire risk** – Damage to property, materials, and assets; loss of life or injuries; excessive insurance premiums.
- **Utility interruptions** – Facility damage or shutdown, critical IT system failures.
- **Explosion** – Damage to property, materials, and assets; loss of life or injuries.
- **Nuclear and radiological risk** – Fallout, inability to access facilities, loss of life or injuries.
- **Hazardous chemicals** – Remediation requirements for chemical spills, inability to access facilities, loss of life or injuries.
- **Infectious disease outbreak** – Governmental mandated shutdown, lack of available resources, changes in consumer demands, inability to manufacture remotely, significant loss of staff.
- **Hurricane, typhoon, and tsunami** – Damage to property, materials, and assets; loss of life or injuries; supply chain interruptions when suppliers are located within potential zones.
- **Flooding** – Inability to access facilities; exposure to finished goods, computer rooms, and controls located on lower levels.

- **Severe winds** – Facility closure; damage to property, materials, and assets; loss of life or injuries.
- **Ice and snowstorms** – Utility issues, freezing pipes, inability to access facilities.
- **Lightning strikes** – Fires, IT equipment damage, associate injuries.
- **Supplier risk** – Force majeure, unavailability of single or sole source supplier.
- **IT service continuity risk** – Unavailability of IT equipment and applications.
- **Communication and media impact** – Loss of market share due to negative external media coverage, reputational damage.
- **Climate change** – Financial impact due to compliance with environmental, social, and governance requirements.

Annual Incident Tracking Process

Documenting the occurrence of actual incidents across all operations increases the likelihood that you will be able to effectively plan for future events and improve response capabilities. Let's review an effective way to track actual incidents across your organization as seen in Table 5.2. Gathering the information below helps determine the accuracy of risk assessments and provides input into planning for your top operational risks.

Table 5.2 Global incident tracking

Region of Origin: Select A, B, C, D	Location	Date Occurred	Incident: Type or Category	Description: Impact, Activities Underway	Duration: Day, Week, Month	Type: Major or Minor

Background Data – Include the following information when tracking major incidents, crises, and business continuity events:

- Date notified.
- Region of occurrence.
- Location details.
- Description of activity.

Type of Hazard or Event – Include the appropriate event category for consistency in reporting. Consider using the following FEMA definitions of hazards:

- Human includes strike, violence, riot, terrorism, hazardous material incident, etc.
- Natural includes natural disasters such as hurricanes, typhoons, flooding, earthquakes, volcanic activity, etc.
- Technological includes power outages, structural failures, attacks on computer networks and systems, etc.

Duration – Select an appropriate category of time the business was impacted, such as:

- Less than one day.
- Between one day and one week.
- More than one week.

Incident Category – Include whether the reportable incident or event is within the range of what the organization's policy classifies as being either major or minor.

Aligned Top Operational Risks

Our manufacturing organization with four business units combined their annual risk assessment and incident reporting data. Feedback from benchmarking with similar organizations, investors, and auditors was also included. An analysis of the greatest operational exposures revealed the top operational risks. The six top operational risks for the organization we highlight throughout the book are listed below. This list can become part of your annual campaign to ensure effective planning for the risks exists with heightened awareness across all levels of the organization.

The top operational risks for our manufacturing organization with four business units are:

Natural Incidents – All natural incidents have the potential to cause significant impacts to the organization's associates, facilities, and business operations. Because the incidents are geographical, they cannot be avoided.

Proactive planning for them is a part of operational resilience. Climatological concerns are constantly being raised by investors and are part of sustainable planning.

Facility and Infrastructure Failure – The ability of the organization to manufacture finished goods can be affected by issues within the facility or services required to meet production schedules. Issues with equipment reliability, facility fires, utility interruptions, and the inability of associates to access or work as expected are included in this risk.

IT System's Impact – IT systems are heavily relied upon to effectively communicate and for critical applications to manufacture products. This risk includes impacts from cyber issues and ransomware events.

Supply Chain Resilience – The ongoing effects of infectious disease, pent up demand, and global sourcing continue to make supply chain disruptions a top operational risk. We include sourcing of materials, logistics, and transportation of raw materials and finished goods in this category of risk.

Geopolitical Risk – Human element issues such as war, political events, protests, and violence are included in this category.

People (Talent) Impact – The lack of alternates in critical roles, including their training and readiness to immediately step in and support the organization, is a concern.

Critical Processes Identified

We will highlight multiple steps to identify and analyze your critical processes through a BIA. Like the Ready Business Risk Assessment Process, we will reference the ready.gov overview of a BIA[4] along with supplemental material. You should consider using a process that is also scalable, has easily understood examples, and is maintained current via the links provided above. While the risk assessment process identifies loss scenarios, a BIA determines critical business activities and processes along with the associated resource requirements. A BIA survey includes predicting the consequences of a disruption of business functions and processes and gathers information needed to develop recovery strategies.

BIA Project Plan

Develop a formal project plan outlining how the BIA is tied to operational resilience. Include all the BIA steps that support your operations. Identify all the stakeholders who will be asked to complete the BIA survey. Include an overview of the BIA components, including how the survey will be completed and how you benefit by taking action to support the most critical business processes.

A smaller organization may consider setting up interviews with the stakeholders. A software-based BIA survey is the most efficient way to survey business leaders and key stakeholders across all operations in a larger organization. Provide some type of training for completing the BIA regardless of how you manage it. Survey those with detailed knowledge of how the business manufactures its products or provides its services. Ask them to identify the potential impacts if the business function or process that they are responsible for is interrupted. The BIA should also identify efficiencies and resources needed for the business to continue to function at different levels.

Identifying Business Impacts

The BIA should identify the impacts resulting from the disruption of critical business functions and processes. Impacts to consider in our example of a global manufacturer with four business units can include:

- Operational impact.
- Lost sales and income.
- Delayed sales or income.
- Increased expenses (e.g., overtime labor, outsourcing, expediting costs, etc.).
- Regulatory fines.
- Contractual penalties or loss of contractual bonuses.
- Customer dissatisfaction.
- Delay of new business plans.

BIA Timing

The timing of when a business function or process is disrupted can have a significant bearing on the loss sustained. A manufacturing location sustaining damage as it is producing finished goods to a major customer may lose a substantial amount of its yearly sales. A power outage lasting a few minutes would be a minor inconvenience for most businesses, but one lasting for hours could result in significant business losses. A short disruption of production may be overcome by shipping finished goods from a warehouse, but disruption of a product in high demand could have a significant impact.

Identify the point in time when the operational or financial interruption would have the greatest impact. Consider if it might be a certain season, end of a month, quarter, etc. Also include the duration of the interruption or point in time when the operational and or financial impact will occur. Common durations for the BIA can include:

- Less than one hour.
- Greater than one hour.
- Less than eight hours.
- Greater than eight hours.
- Less than 24 hours.
- Less than 72 hours.
- Greater than 72 hours.
- Greater than one week.
- Greater than one month.

Required Data

Here are a few items our global manufacturer should consider including in the BIA:

Locations – Survey all the locations having an upstream or downstream dependency to the processes being surveyed.
Processes – Include all major business processes tied to the locations referenced that are considered critical parts in the manufacturing product flow.
Products – Add products linked to each process.
Applications – Include the applications to run each process.
Vendors – Add any vendors associated with each process.
Resources – Identify how many employees and what type of equipment are needed daily.

BIA Report

The final step in the BIA process is constructing the BIA summary report. The report should include recovery strategies backed by data from your operational business process experts. It's the most important step in the process since the end goal is to help identify the most effective contingency plans to get business recovery underway when needed. Here are a few suggested items to include in the BIA summary report:

- Summary of the how BIA process was implemented.
- BIA scope and objectives.
- BIA findings summary.
- Details of each critical process including:

    o The most important business processes from recovery time perspective.
    o Potential business impacts from disruptions.

- o The Recovery Time Objective (RTO) (i.e., how long the business can withstand the disruption).
- o The Recovery Point Objective (RPO) (i.e., the maximum amount of loss the business can tolerate); and
- o Comparison of costs from downtime to cost for effective recovery strategies.
- Prioritized restoration recommendations with greatest operational and financial impacts being restored first.
- Detailed document summary.
- Suggested actions from the BIA summary.

You have now gathered the appropriate details from your operational business experts and can take the next step toward building plans for an effective recovery.

Impact Tolerance

As you continue toward operational resilience, you will come across other business sectors that are adapting their programs to changing industry regulations. For example, the UK introduced the concept of impact tolerances for financial sectors[5]. The key principle behind setting impact tolerances is to ensure that boards and senior management are preparing for disruptions, whereas traditional risk management focuses on risk avoidance.

Impact tolerance defines the Maximum Tolerable Level of Disruption (MTLD)[6] to a critical business service which is the point in time following the disruptive event where your organization will be severely impacted if the critical business service is not resumed. You can follow a similar process as with the BIA to validate readiness and resilience aligned with the MTLD. Consider conducting the evaluation on an annual basis or more frequently, based on changing business conditions.

Let's outline a few steps to consider with the impact tolerance process:

Identify Important Business Services

Consider starting by contacting the same team members who provided the critical business processes to identify important business services. Conduct a survey that includes the processes, technology, people, information, facilities, and anything else involved in maintaining the business services. Include what you've identified as the RTO and the RPO from your BIA in the impact tolerance analysis.

Here are a few factors to consider when identifying critical business services:

- Financial stability.
- Potential for reputational impact.
- Legal impacts.
- Regulatory impacts.

Impact Tolerance Metrics

Once you have your list of most critical business services, identify the metrics and baseline for your MTLD analysis. Have at least one impact tolerance level for each business service identified. You can use the same time-based metrics you used for the BIA. Another metric can be volumes of materials or transactions related to the time-based metrics. This will identify how the organization can tolerate a shortage of materials or transactions for a certain number of hours or days. Do not include the frequency of occurrences—just the impact from a single occurrence.

Steps to Stay Within Impact Tolerances

Once you've identified critical business services and MTLDs, define the steps needed for your organization to continue to deliver important business services. The goal is to stay within the defined impact tolerances. Consider using business continuity planning and other tools we identified as being of value in your toolbox to help stay within impact tolerances for your operations. We will highlight business continuity planning next.

Impact Tolerance Testing

Once plans are developed, they should be tested frequently to remain within impact tolerances. You can begin testing your plans through tabletop exercises as we reviewed in this book. The testing should include evaluating realistic scenarios that assess your ability to remain within defined impact tolerances. Items to include during scenario testing include:

- Failures of planning whether within your direct control or not.
- Exposing critical business services to the top operational risks you previously identified.
- Availability of resources to support the impact tolerances.
- Assumptions in determining effectiveness of actions.
- Dependencies on materials, customers, and related processes.
- Dependencies on team members executing critical tasks.
- Documents that are necessary and available to maintain services.
- An after-action summary of key takeaways and objectives that must be completed to maintain impact tolerances.

Any gaps identified in plan testing should be included in your continuous improvement process. This impact tolerance example goes a long way in building your team's operational resilience training and knowledge. Ensure you have a process that clearly identifies who is responsible, accountable, consulted, and informed on the key takeaways from each impact tolerance testing exercise.

Business Continuity Plans, Playbooks and Documentation

Forward thinking organizations follow a formal process to complete their annual calendar of business continuity activities. They first conduct a risk assessment to determine the top operational risks, then they complete a BIA to determine their most critical business processes. Finally, they develop business continuity plans. Let's include details on constructing business continuity plans, regardless of the size of your organization.

Not every facility in your operations has the capability to build a detailed business continuity plan, because an effective plan requires the use of software which may be complicated and time consuming to learn. In addition, smaller facilities may not have the staffing to develop detailed business continuity plans. Below are suggestions for documenting planning based on staffing levels at your facilities. It's divided into three scalable types of plans depending on how many associates work at the facility, balanced by the criticality of their business functions. When software is used, be sure to provide as much training and support as possible.

Business Continuity Planning Documentation

As a minimum, every region should develop a strategy that cascades to all of their facilities, including manufacturing and non-manufacturing operations. Manufacturing facilities may be seen as more critical to the success of the business, so consider having them all complete formal business continuity plans. Non-manufacturing facilities which may include retail stores, logistic operations, regional headquarters, data centers, local offices, etc., should prepare a more basic version of a plan. Let's establish requirements for completing business continuity plans based on the number of associates and contractors working at each facility. The numbers below are scalable.

Staffing from 1-49 Individuals – Develop and maintain a business continuity one-pager document as outlined below that is closely aligned with your regional operations team.

Staffing from 50-199 Individuals – Develop and maintain a business continuity playbook as outlined below that is closely aligned with your regional operations team.

Staffing from 200 or More Individuals – Develop and maintain a business continuity plan as outlined below that is closely aligned with your regional operations team.

Critical Facilities – If a facility or location is identified as being a critical regional location, regardless of staffing size, they should develop and maintain a Business Continuity Plan as outlined below that is closely aligned with your regional operations team.

Business Continuity One-Pager

The business continuity one-pager is the most basic document every one of your facilities should maintain on site, share with key personnel, and have ready as a reference document. It provides the local team's guidance on steps to take when managing an incident, crisis, or a business continuity event. The information below can be part of the one-pager to maintain a strong alignment between their location and their regional team. The one-pager consists of the front and back of a page but can be expanded by some locations into a multiple page document if the region wants to include additional alignment information.

- Initial actions in support of associates.
- Incident response roles and responsibilities.
- Method of reporting incidents to their regions.
- Method of notifying associates and team members.
- Guidance on communications and social media.
- List of external authorities to engage by type of crisis or event.
- List of contractors to contact for local support.
- Guidance on top local risks requiring local planning.
- Critical business processes requiring immediate support.
- How to document activities until regional support is underway.
- Location of and links to additional supporting documents.

Business Continuity Playbook

A business continuity playbook contains more of the strategies, tactics, and methods to follow than the business continuity one-pager does but does not have the amount of information your formal business continuity plan does. In addition to the items in the business continuity one-pager, consider supplementing your business continuity playbook with the additional content below:

- Team scope and structure.
- Major incident reporting and management details.
- Method for notifying response team.

- Method of communicating with all associates.
- How and when to initiate the playbook.
- Guidance on managing the incident.
- Details on operating protocols.
- How to determine whether an event will be managed by local incident response, business continuity, or crisis management team.
- Post-incident gap analysis and process improvement.
- Additional resources, such as:

  o Incident response plan.
  o Incident action lists.
  o Site specific details.
  o Awareness and training.
  o Media and crisis communications contacts.

Business Continuity Plan

As we did with the risk assessment and BIA, the business continuity plan information below includes material which was taken directly from the ready.gov BC Plan website[7]. This is a general overview of what's in a business continuity plan. You can reference the foregoing link for additional details or work with a business continuity software provider to determine your best course of action to maintain your journey. Consider using this as a starting point for business continuity planning with our global manufacturer example.

Development of a business continuity plan includes four steps:

1) Identify your top operational risks through an organizational risk assessment process.
2) Conduct a BIA to identify time-sensitive or critical business functions and processes and the resources that support them.
3) Organize a business continuity team and compile a business continuity plan to manage business disruption.
4) Conduct training for the business continuity team and testing with exercises to evaluate recovery strategies and the plan.

IT programs and applications require special focus. They have many components such as networks, servers, desktop and laptop computers, and wireless devices. The ability to run both office productivity and enterprise software is critical. Therefore, IT recovery strategies should be developed so technology can be restored in time to meet the needs of the business. In addition, manual workarounds should be part of the IT plan so business can continue while computer systems are being restored.

Recovery of a critical or time-sensitive process requires resources. In order to determine what resources will be needed to carry out recovery strategies and restore normal business operations, a business continuity resource requirements worksheet needs to be completed by business function and process managers. Resources can come from within the business or be provided by third parties. Resources include:

- Employees.
- Office space, furniture, and equipment.
- Technology (e.g., computers, peripherals, communication equipment, software and data).
- Vital records (electronic and hard copy).
- Production facilities, machinery, and equipment.
- Inventory, including raw materials, finished goods, and goods in production.
- Utilities (e.g., power, natural gas, water, sewer, telephone, internet, and wireless).
- Third party services.

Since all resources cannot be replaced immediately following a loss, your teams should estimate the resources that will be needed in the hours, days, and weeks following an incident.

Recovery strategies are priorities for restoration of business processes and should be identified in the business continuity plan. Recovery strategies are alternate means to restore business operations to a minimum acceptable level following a business disruption and are prioritized by the RTO and the RPO developed during the BIA. Primary and dependent resource requirements should also be identified.

Recovery strategies require resources including people, facilities, equipment, materials, and information technology. An analysis of the resources required to execute recovery strategies should be conducted to identify gaps. For example, if a machine fails but other machines are readily available to make up lost production, then there is no resource gap. However, if all machines are lost due to a flood, and insufficient undamaged inventory is available to meet customer demand until production is restored, production might be made up by machines at another facility—whether owned or contracted. Strategies may involve contracting with third parties, entering into partnership or reciprocal agreements, or displacing other activities within the company. Staff with in-depth knowledge of business functions and processes are in the best position to determine what will work. Possible alternatives should be explored and presented to management for approval and to decide how much to spend.

Depending upon the size of the company and resources available, there may be many recovery strategies that can be explored. Utilization of other owned or controlled facilities performing similar work is one option. Operations may be relocated to an alternate site, assuming both are not impacted by the same incident. This strategy also assumes that the surviving site has the resources and capacity to assume the work of the impacted site. Prioritization of production or service levels, providing additional staff and resources and other action would be needed if capacity at the second site is inadequate.

Telecommuting is a strategy employed when staff can work from home through remote connectivity. It can be used in combination with other strategies to reduce alternate site requirements. This strategy requires ensuring telecommuters have a suitable work environment and are equipped with or have access to a computer with required applications and data, peripherals, and a secure broadband connection. In an emergency, space at another facility can be put to use. Cafeterias, conference rooms, and training rooms can be converted to office space or to other uses when needed. Equipping converted space with furnishings, equipment, power, connectivity, and other resources would be required to meet the needs of workers.

Partnership or reciprocal agreements can be arranged with other businesses or organizations that can support each other in the event of a disaster. Assuming space is available, issues such as the capacity and connectivity of telecommunications and information technology, protection of privacy and intellectual property, the impacts to each other's operation and allocating expenses must be addressed. Agreements should be negotiated in writing and documented in the business continuity plan. Periodic review of the agreement is needed to determine if there is a change in the ability of each party to support the other.

There are many vendors that support business continuity and information technology recovery strategies. External suppliers can provide a full business environment including office space and live data centers that are ready to be occupied. Other options include technology equipped office trailers, replacement machinery, and other equipment. The availability and cost of these options can be affected when a regional disaster results in competition for these resources.

Use of existing owned or leased facilities. Multiple strategies for recovery of manufacturing operations include:

- Shifting production from one facility to another.
- Increasing manufacturing output at operational facilities.
- Retooling production from one item to another.
- Prioritizing production—by profit margin or customer relationship.

- Maintaining higher inventory of raw materials or finished goods.
- Reallocating existing inventory or repurchasing or buying back inventory.
- Limiting orders (e.g., maximum order size or unit quantity).
- Contracting with third parties.
- Purchasing business interruption insurance.

Additional factors in manufacturing recovery strategies include:

- Will a facility be available when needed?
- How much time will it take to shift production from one product to another?
- How much will it cost to shift production from one product to another?
- How much revenue would be lost when displacing other production?
- How much extra time will it take to receive raw materials or ship finished goods to customers? Will the extra time impact customer relationships?
- Are there any regulations that would restrict shifting production?
- What quality issues could arise if production is shifted or outsourced?
- Are there any long-term consequences associated with a strategy?

Manual workarounds should be identified as a backup to primary recovery planning. The following should be considered as part of the information and workflow:

- Internal interfaces (e.g., department, person, activity, and resource requirements).
- External interfaces (e.g., company, contact person, activity, and resource requirements).
- Tasks (in sequential order).
- Manual intervention points.
- The creation of data collection forms to capture information and define processes for manual handling of the information collected.
- The establishment of control logs to document transactions and track their progress through the manual system.
- Reassignment of staff or temporary assistance to cover the manual labor required by workarounds.

We have provided quite a bit of information on business continuity plans, playbooks and one-pagers. Having a scalable way of aligning all facilities across the region is required to maintain readiness, response, and continuous improvement across your operations.

Maintaining Progress

We've provided concepts to assist in the identification, execution, and process improvement of resilient deployment strategies. Keeping your team members actively engaged helps promote support and understanding of these concepts. We know meetings impact everyone's blocks of work, so we want to ensure that we produce effective results when teams meet. Let's review some steps for running effective and productive meetings to support resilient deployment.

How to Run Successful Resilient Deployment Meetings

Having meetings to ensure you function well as a team is an important part of resilience deployment. Take the time needed to plan, execute, and improve on team activities for the benefit of your entire organization. Let's review suggested steps to ensure your meetings are most effective.

Focus on the results – You want everyone invited to be looking forward to attending your meetings, knowing their time will be went spent, their input will be valued, and they will be contributors in making progress on the resilience journey. All participants should attend or send alternates to provide their input. Those not invited yet who are part of resilient deployment should be made aware they will be invited when they add value to the specific meeting in respect of everyone's time. Be sure that everyone who attends believes they are given a chance to share their ideas on important topics. When you create meaningful discussions with everyone during meetings, it can help improve morale and increase productivity. The entire organization will be aware of the positive reputation your meetings have for creating well aligned and focused results.

Steps to ensure success – Let's review a few suggested steps to help you manage a successful meeting.

- Establish the goal of your meeting and how it supports your roadmap and your project planning.
- Set the meeting agenda and develop documents to be shared in advance with the meeting participants.
- Determine the optimum time for the meeting, taking regional time zones into account and avoiding meetings over lunch hours, evenings, Friday afternoon, or backing up to holidays and known vacation times.
- Consider starting your meeting on the hour and ending it five minutes prior to standard calendar times to avoid overlapping meetings.
- Only invite those who are expected to contribute to the agenda—others who only need to be informed of the results should not be invited.
- Send the meeting invitation in advance, allowing attendees to respond and plan for how they will contribute to the agenda.

- Start the meeting on time, monitor progress throughout the meeting, and conclude on time.
- Keep participants focused on the meeting's agenda, steering the team away from discussions not connected to the main topics.
- Be aware of challenges created by virtual meetings and keep everyone on topic and participative.
- Be prepared for potential issues by logging in early, testing the technology, and having a backup plan if issues arise.
- Document action items from the meeting directly or with support from one of the participants.
- Distribute the meeting results and action items to the participants and others who may be affected by the results.
- Set the next meeting date and time and send the invitation to all participants.
- Consider surveying your participants occasionally to get their feedback on whether the meeting added value, whether they were the right team members to be invited, and whether they have any suggested improvements to achieve better results.

Suggested Resilience Team Meeting Frequencies and Agenda

Let's review how often the teams we've established for our example organization should meet, what they should cover, and how this benefits resilient deployment. See Table 5.3 for an example of how meetings can help align teams across your operations.

Table 5.3 Team alignment

Team Alignment	Meeting Frequency	Topics Reviewed
Global and Individual Regional Leaders	Weekly	Progress to AOP
Global and All Regional Leaders	Monthly	Progress to AOP and sharing of best practices
Global, Regional and Operational Leadership	Quarterly	ABCs of Operational Resilience
Regions and Facility Teams	Monthly	Progress to AOP
Regions, Tactical and Facility Teams	Quarterly	ABCs of Operational Resilience
Global and Tactical Team	Quarterly	ABCs of Operational Resilience
Global and Governance Committee	Quarterly	Progress to AOP and Strategic Alignment
Global Resilient Strategy Overview	Annual	Alignment on Current AOP, Long- and Short-Term Project Plan

Global meetings should occur as follows:

- Weekly between the global leader and individual regional leaders. A brief check-in on progress toward aligning with global and regional AOP helps maintain momentum. This is a good opportunity for the participants to quickly address any minor issues or concerns and bring in others for feedback, if needed.
- Monthly between the global and all regional leaders can focus on the AOP, any relevant business continuity events or crises, and benchmarking of relevance.
- Quarterly between the global leader, all regional leaders, and operational leadership. Consider the concept of using the Activities, Best Practices and Crises (ABCs) of business continuity as the topic of discussion. The regional leaders should provide a formal update to all participants in this meeting.
- Quarterly between the global leader and global tactical support functions can be held to keep all teams well engaged on their annual objectives.
- Quarterly between the global leader and the Governance Committee helps maintain the strategic direction of all teams and gets support to overcome obstacles with support from top level leaders, if needed.

Regional meetings should occur as follows:

- Monthly with every one of their major operational facilities. Like the global meeting, the discussion can focus on the AOP, any relevant business continuity events or crises, and benchmarking the participants benefit by.
- Quarterly between the regional leader, all facility leaders, tactical team members, and operational leadership. Include the concept of the ABCs of business continuity as the topic of discussion. The facility and tactical leaders should provide a formal update to all participants in this meeting.

Annual resilient deployment reviews can be held each calendar year. Consider holding them in the fourth quarter and reviewing progress made in the present calendar year and setting aligned strategies per the project plan for the upcoming year. Include a review of the items below. The results and targets for the upcoming year should be shared with all regional and facility team members.

- Progress toward the project plan, including what's working, what's not, and where help is needed.

- Annual quantitative and qualitative scorecard results.
- Calendar of events completed, including all activities, awareness, training, testing, and continuous improvement.
- Maturity model results with a continued focus on a three-year target of improvement.
- Top operational risk comparison with survey risk results, actual crises and business continuity events, and trending risks for the upcoming year.

How to Lead, Follow and Guide the Way With Resilient Deployment

Resilient Deployment is a formal process where all operational teams follow a common method to plan, execute, verify, and improve on activities tied to operational resilience. The concepts and strategies below should be completed and tracked for success across the organization.

o **Develop and maintain a documented project plan with well-defined short- and long-term goals and objectives.** Create a purpose statement and build your project around it. Look at three-year strategic goals, what can be done in two years, and immediate priorities. Align immediate (current year) objectives across the organization. Make the objectives simple and SMART.

o **Use a scorecard to track progress toward primary objectives.** Track progress monthly to both qualitative and quantitative targets. Include the most important operational calendar-based activities, how teams respond to crises, and audit results. Your combined scorecard reflects what your teams accomplished and how well they are executing.

o **Identify and focus on your top operations risks.** Analyze results from your risk surveys, regionally reported incidents, and trending global risks. Have an effective method for every associate across the organization to report and manage major incidents. Do a monthly check in on the status of progress in planning for your top operational risks.

o **Implement business continuity planning with all operational facilities.** In addition to overall risk management, conduct an annual BIA and build business continuity plans. Share results with team participants and leadership. Have a scalable plan with business continuity one-pagers, playbooks and formal plans based on facility criticality and capability of teams to complete them. Consider reviewing the organization's impact tolerances by identifying maximum tolerable levels of downtime.

o **Maintain progress by keeping teams across all levels of your organizations aligned.** Take steps to help manage successful meetings. Set the right meeting frequencies, invite the right attendees, and create productive agendas. Include an annual cadence of meetings for global, regional, facility, tactical, and leadership teams.

How to Lead

Develop an organizational team, your project plan, and a scorecard to help track progress toward current year results. Summarize the top operational risks, your critical business processes, and how you plan to recover. Establish a well aligned series of resilience meetings between relevant teams. Share the proposed deployment plans with regional operational leadership.

How to Follow

Consolidate feedback from key stakeholders on all activities related to resilient deployment. Benchmark with relevant customers and industry best practices. Modify your resilient deployment activities based on internal and external feedback, along with what may be of value to your teams.

How to Guide the Way

- Manage execution of resilience deployment activities with ongoing feedback from regional leadership and counterparts.
- Stay consistently focused on the organization's mission and objectives, along with risks that can affect them.
- Look for the right timing to engage others who have a common vision.
- Eliminate complexity as you develop clarity by communicating easily understood goals.
- Get the right balance between what may be too much or too little.
- Let everyone know you value their input and that the process is team-based and jointly developed, and then build on the energy created with your team.
- Continue to modify your roadmap and remain focused on continuous improvement.

Notes

1 https://www.ready.gov/
2 https://www.ready.gov/risk-assessment
3 https://www.ready.gov/business
4 https://www.ready.gov/business-impact-analysis

5 The Bank of England, 'Supervisory Statement | SS1/21 – Operational resilience: Impact tolerances for important business services', March 2022, https://www.bankofengland.co.uk/-/media/boe/files/prudential-regulation/supervisory-statement/2021/ss121-march-22.pdf

6 BCM Institute, 'Maximum Tolerable Level of Disruption', https://www.bcmpedia.org/wiki/Maximum_Tolerable_Level_of_Disruption

7 https://www.ready.gov/business-continuity-plan

Chapter VI

Objectives Overcome Obstacles

Common objectives that are well defined, communicated, and understood will help support your organization's mission. These objectives should be followed by all your operational team members and aligned with your short- and long-term planning. In this chapter, we will review concepts to assist in the identification, execution, and improvement process of resilient deployment strategies covered in Chapter 5. We will also include how personal resilience and behaviors help inspire executing objectives.

- Common Obstacles to Meeting Objectives
- Annual Objective Setting
- Global and Regional Leader Objectives
- Operational Team Objectives
- Blocks of Work
- Progress Reporting
- Actions to Improve Engagement
- Leadership Mindset

Common Obstacles to Meeting Objectives

Wouldn't it be great if we could set objectives by identifying and prioritizing them, knowing they will be completed as expected? Although it does sound quite simple, there are a few obstacles to meeting this expectation. Let's review some of the issues you may run into when attempting to meet objectives, along with suggestions on how to overcome them.

The Process of Setting Objectives is Not Understood

Every company has a way to set objectives for their people and their teams. It's important for you to follow the process your organization uses in setting and approving objectives and tracking their results. Top leadership sets operational objectives. They receive input and buy in from multiple stakeholders.

DOI: 10.4324/9781003438700-6

Human resources teams help manage and advise you on how to set objectives. The objectives should be specific and measurable and should help drive expected results. They should be tied to the talent management process including compensation, performance, development, and succession planning. Every objective should be tracked and measured. Keep in mind that the objectives should be long-term commitments to support operational resilience, not short-term solutions.

The objective setting process should include getting feedback from associates and teams on any issues they see that could hinder objectives being successfully completed. They should not be afraid to speak up and should believe they can provide suggestions to improve the organization. This allows them to recognize and report concerns and maintain a continuous-improvement mindset. Your associates have unique backgrounds and experiences that can benefit the entire organization. Be aware of these benefits and the advantages they provide during your planning process.

The Objectives Are Not Clearly Defined

It benefits all stakeholders to be transparent and communicate effectively throughout the objective setting and management process. Every team member needs current-year objectives that tie back to your overall short- and long-term project planning. If the objectives are not clearly defined, they can cause confusion and lack of clarity across all levels of the organization. If there are too many or conflicting goals, they can create or promote a lack of focus and discipline. Teams may end up working in silos with associates doing "busy work" that does not promote moving their operations toward resilience. For those reasons, ensure you've followed the documented project plan as explained in our resilient deployment process.

There is No Commitment to Completing Objectives

You can tell if someone states they want to achieve common team objectives, but they are not truly committed. Their actions in not giving it their best effort may show they don't have the same interest other team members have in doing what's needed. Commitment is crucial to your goal to meet desired objectives—without it, you will encounter mediocre outcomes. Once again, by following your project plan as defined in your resilient deployment process, it quickly becomes evident who shares the necessary team commitment to succeed.

When team members hold one another accountable for delivering results, they share a common goal of meeting and exceeding their joint objectives.

That commitment is what's needed to attain desired results and promote continuous improvement.

The significance of behavioral competencies cannot be overlooked. Situational awareness and promoting collaboration leverage better outcomes. Being agile enables you to take quick action with better results. Energized teams are motivated, empowered, and inspired and will promote your progress.

Time Is an Issue

Let's remember the importance of not overloading anyone's blocks of work. Most participants in your operational resilience process are part-time, not full-time equivalents. Part-time and full-time equivalent are terms typically used by human resources and accounting personnel. They reference the term in making calculations for benchmarking revenues, calculating various metrics, and determining how laws may apply in an organization. We use these terms to determine how resources are allocated to help meet operational resilience goals and objectives. Most often it's better to have full-time equivalents in the roles we've discussed, but you can still meet objectives with part-time personnel.

Regardless of the type of team support you have, having too many objectives may misdirect your teams. They may choose objectives that are easier to achieve, more desirable to work on, and not necessarily the goals that are of greatest operational value. In addition, having too many objectives may cause your teams to rush and take shortcuts that could cause safety risks. Overloading your teams with multiple priorities can also hinder their expectations of success. The goal is to balance workloads and to stay in line with changing short-term operational goals. If you receive feedback indicating that there are too many goals and objectives, focus on primary ones that provide the highest return on effort. Once they are completed, then focus on remaining priorities in order of importance.

Lack of Leadership Support

When direct managers and operational leaders are on board with objectives promoting resilience, their teams will receive the right level of support, and the odds of successfully achieving objectives will increase. Approach your teams in advance of setting objectives and demonstrate how they are part of your project plan which is closely aligned with the organization's mission. Show how there is a beneficial return on the time, energy, and resources invested in reaching objectives. Direct managers and leadership can also help tie objectives to employee development programs and succession planning. Get them to energize the team by recognizing those who deliver results by performing well in completing objectives. Work together to demonstrate how the roles supporting operational resilience are considered positive development opportunities for future leaders.

Annual Objective Setting

Your company's mission and vision can be converted into objectives and goals all associates can somehow support. They begin with high-level goals set by your senior leadership team and cascade throughout the organization. Various departments such as human resources should help set a timeframe for annual objective goal setting. Many of the goals are strategic and address these questions:

1. Do they help accomplish the mission statement?
2. Are they linked to improving competitive advantage?
3. Will they expand sales, create new markets, or support research and development?
4. Are they focused on growth in revenues, earnings, and profit margins?
5. Do they improve present purchasing, logistics, transportation, and supply chain programs?

You better the odds of improving objectives across an organization by focusing on what's working, what needs improvement, and why. Well-written objectives provide clear direction for your associates. They can promote quick decision making and maintain alignment toward operational goals. The objectives should be written so managers and associates can clearly review and measure their progress. Although most organizations recommend mid-year and annual check-ins, I recommend a monthly review of progress on objectives. We've discussed the importance of making every objective SMART. Since we are providing examples of objectives for our global manufacturer with four business units, let's recap how to keep your team's objectives SMART.

- **Specific** objectives are clearly understood, precise, and detailed. They are focused on actions and outcomes and contain action verbs. They are not vague or simply a checklist of a job description.
- **Measurable** objectives can be tracked and are tied to results in measurable intervals. They should include specific actions and metrics.
- **Attainable** objectives are achievable but not too easy to reach. They should include a reasonable time to accomplish them which will motivate your teams to complete them on schedule.

- **Relevant** objectives are closely aligned with operational resilience goals. Everyone should know that success in attaining personal goals means success in attaining business goals.
- **Time-bound** objectives identify a time frame for their accomplishment. They are not open ended and should have a sense of urgency for their completion.

A study by Gartner[1] reviews nine steps to successful functional strategic planning. The study reveals only 29 percent of organizations change plans fast enough to respond to disruption. By following a methodical step-by-step approach, you can maintain clarity from setting expectations through communicating objectives, developing action plans, tracking performance, and delivering results.

Global and Regional Leader Objectives

Every team member supporting operational resilience should have well-defined and aligned objectives that are tied to the organization's mission and your project plan. This helps ensure the present year's objectives, goals, and measures are relevant and follow the annual objective setting process. Your global and regional business continuity leaders play a much greater role in operational resilience than their facility or tactical team members. In Chapter 4 we provided suggestions on business continuity leadership roles for a global manufacturer. All the global roles should report directly to the global business continuity leader. We also recommended having regional business continuity leaders report to the global leader through a matrix management process. A matrix organization is designed to deploy resilience strategies in a common way across all regional operations. Through the matrix structure, the global leader has input on the performance of each regional leader's business continuity role in meeting global objectives. Working closely with their direct managers, both the global leader and direct manager can jointly support the objectives and have input in the performance appraisal process.

Global and regional business continuity leaders support the organization by having objectives that are well aligned with both quantitative and qualitative scorecard components. Below are examples of annual objectives with suggested metrics for global and regional leaders. Remember to keep all objectives SMART.

1. **Provide strategic business continuity leadership and support aligned with global initiatives across the entire region throughout the year.**

    a. Percent of calendar-based activities supported by the region (e.g., monthly reporting, surveys, audits, tabletops, etc.).

    b. Percent of requests completed for updates to annual documents, objectives, quarterly reviews, scorecards, etc.

    c. Percent of actual incidents and business continuity events actively managed in the region from escalation through conclusion.

    d. Percent of actual incidents where regional crisis management engagement was needed, and support was provided.

    e. Percent of activities completed for each block of work on a monthly basis.

2. **Complete all activities related to improving regional business continuity maturity level across all regional locations throughout the year. Note that maturity levels will be covered in Chapter 7.**

    a. Participate in 100 percent of activities regarding team training and engagement.

    b. Support objective setting and management for 100 percent of critical team members.

    c. Minimum compliant maturity level reached in all regions by fourth quarter of the year.

3. **Lead regional planning and response activities related to the top operational risks in the region throughout the year.**

    a. Percent of facilities continually engaged with awareness and ready to respond to the top operational risks.

    b. Percent of teams using applicable business continuity plans, playbooks, actions list, etc., to address risks.

4. **Effective use of business continuity software throughout the year.**

    a. Percent of business continuity calendar of activities completed.

    b. Percent of applicable business continuity events managed within software.

    c. Percent of business continuity events and crises documented with software.

Operational Team Objectives

The team members receiving a business continuity objective should be selected by their direct managers and approved by global and regional leaders. They will represent the facility and tactical functions that are relied upon in planning for, responding to, recovering from, and improving upon activities promoting operational resilience. Determine which functional roles are most important and have primary and alternate team members who show interest and are ready to provide their expertise and support. Every year I meet with our corporate executive human resources leader and jointly send a message to our team members who will receive an annual objective.

Our human resources leader along with regional leaders support the objectives. We provide a single objective with metrics that identify how we will measure success in completing them throughout the year. The objective includes their expected participation during incidents, crises, and business continuity events. Because the time required to successfully complete the objective can be significant, direct management support is needed. Below is an example of a well-defined common operational team member objective.

Our Request of You as Critical Business Continuity Team Associates:

- Review, reflect upon, and align with your direct managers and commit to this important objective throughout the year.
- Align with your direct management to objectively evaluate your performance per this objective.
- Participate as outlined below.
- Be aware of and support your team in executing the roles and responsibilities as needed.
- Contact your regional or global business continuity leader for additional details.

Objective:

- Active and engaged contributor and team representative for the business continuity process in support of operational resilience.

Metrics:

- Gain sign-off and acknowledgement from your manager of your business continuity responsibilities by the end of January.
- Participate in appropriate business continuity training by the end of the first quarter, and actively participate in meetings and training programs throughout the year.
- Attend and actively participate in appropriate business continuity meetings and training programs throughout the year as measured by your attendance.
- Ensure 100 percent of all surveys, assignments, and feedback requested is completed on or before assigned completion dates.
- Engage appropriate leadership (manufacturing or non-manufacturing) in the performance of business continuity activities (including risk assessments, business impact analysis, plans, events, crises, audits, and business continuity maturity surveys) throughout the year.

Blocks of Work

In preparing for the journey with your roadmap, we referenced blocks of work as a great way to identify the time commitments to attain resilience. To create a blocks of work summary, begin by preparing a spreadsheet listing the most important activities throughout each month as seen in Table 6.1. Your monthly blocks of work should align with your scorecard reporting. Monthly progress reporting allows time to complete activities while you balance priorities. If you experience an issue that stalls performance, you have enough time to correct it in subsequent months and still make progress throughout the year. Include the most significant activities and tasks that are part of your journey. All the short-term objectives in your project planning should be included (e.g., meetings, training, plan

Table 6.1 Monthly blocks of work document

Monthly Blocks of Work Document

Activities Requiring Time Commitment (Itemize with as much detail as possible)	Time in Hours for Each Activity							
	Daily	*Weekly*	*Monthly*	*Quarterly*	*Semi Annually*	*Annually*	*As Needed*	*Monthly Total*
Meetings								
Training								
Risk Assessment								
Business Impact Analysis								
Business Continuity Plans								
Business Continuity Playbooks								
Business Continuity One-Pagers								
Tabletop Exercises								
Communication Articles								
Newsletters								
Audits								
Maturity Surveys								
Benchmarking								
Incident Response								
Business Continuity Events								
Crisis Management								

Monthly Blocks of Work Analysis:
Maximum monthly work hours:
80% of monthly work hours:
Hours required for activities this month:
Hours exceeding 80% of monthly work hours limit:
Actions required to remain within 80% of monthly work hours:

development, documentation, testing, etc.). Also include an estimate of the hours you will spend supporting global or regional responses to incidents, crises, and business continuity events. Don't forget about the work involved in post-event gap analysis surveys, documentation, and process improvement activities. You can build upon this summary to also include the deliverables from each significant activity.

By comparing the actual or expected hours needed to address every commitment, you will quickly see if you have time for other activities or if you need to reassess your priorities. This analysis can help you approach management and request additional personnel support in completing operational priorities. Ideally, keeping the maximum expected time commitment to 80 percent of the time you work allows for additional unexpected activities to also be successfully completed. Table 6.1 is an example of a basic blocks of work summary for one month which you can expand for the entire year.

Progress Reporting and Reinforcing Core Competency Behaviors

You've identified the global, regional, and tactical team members who should participate in the annual objective setting process across the organization. They are aware of the importance of supporting operational resilience and what is expected of them throughout the year. They should have ongoing dialogue with their direct managers and fellow team members during meetings, training, and progress check ins. The blocks of work analysis includes time commitments required to be a successful team member. In addition, the appropriate objectives should be part of your mid-year and end-of-year progress reviews and rating process. Direct managers of those who have the common objectives in critical operational supporting roles should be aware of the required time commitments. They should also ask for updates on the incidents, crises, and business continuity events their team members have been involved in during one-on-one meetings and in team meetings. Let's recap how the five core competency behaviors we see as supporting success can be reinforced during mid-year progress check-ins and end-of-year performance reviews.

Situational Awareness

Every team member should be aware of how they are asked to support the team and focus on the right activities. All team members should know when to make the team's needs a priority over other work. You will minimize the impact of a risk and avoid a crisis when your team reacts with a purpose when risks are escalating. The goal remains to support the most appropriate work stream during a business continuity event.

Agility

Being agile allows you to take actions with speed and purpose and enables you to quickly adjust to changing conditions. You will deal with many unknowns during crises and business continuity events. Taking quick action benefits the team by turning opportunities into results which in turn helps fellow team members gain confidence and make better group decisions. By helping to stabilize the team during extreme challenges, you will see improved productivity, efficiencies, and motivation levels.

Promoting Collaboration

Teams perform more effectively when you have open dialogue and you distribute credit appropriately so that individuals who provided significant contributions are rewarded. Be sure to seek out and consider others' ideas and perspectives to support team resilience. Simplifying all actions and key takeaways will improve the team's response.

Energizing the Team

Your overall team response will improve when all team members are empowered to make key contributions. Your entire team will be energized when each member is able to contribute with their unique skills and abilities. Take the time to regularly celebrate progress and success.

Delivering Results

Every incident, crisis, and event creates opportunities to not only achieve business goals, but to build capabilities for the future. By focusing on achieving goals, beating deadlines, and executing excellence, you better the odds of consistently delivering the right results. Remember that your goal includes thriving from challenges and attaining a competitive advantage over your competitors.

Actions to Improve Engagement

In our review of how to effectively align teams, we suggested having a regularly scheduled time to check in with global, regional, and facility team members. We've outlined some of the many benefits of conducting productive meetings. Consider having a quarterly review with your teams on their progress toward their annual objectives. You can ask every team represented (primary and alternate team members) to complete a document and be prepared to discuss their ABCs including incidents or business continuity events) from the past quarter. See Table 6.2 for a template you

Table 6.2 Quarterly meetings

Region A Quarterly Operational Resilience Review

Attended Review	Team/Function	Quarterly Team Update
✓	Communications	
✓	Environment, Health, Safety and Sustainability	
✓	Finance	
✓	Engineering	
✓	Health and Medical	
✓	HR	
✓	IT	
✓	Legal	
✓	Logistics	
✓	Procurement	
✓	Quality	
✓	Risk Management	
✓	Security	
✓	Supply Chain	
✓	Facility 1	
✓	Facility 2	
✓	Facility 3	

Key Takeaways:

1.
2.
3.
4.
5.

can use for one of the global manufacturing regions. Send it to all the meeting participants well in advance so they can reach out to other team members, consolidate information, and ensure it is an accurate summary of their quarterly progress. Invite your operational leadership and ask them to provide a leadership message and their feedback on the results of the meeting. Distribute the final document to all attendees after the meeting along with any takeaways or action items coming out of the team review. Repeat this quarterly in support of your annual objective.

Leadership Mindset

Our introduction focused on the importance of personal resilience as a contributor to your success in attaining operational resilience. We described a resilient person as someone who thrives through challenges and is strong, persistent, tenacious, and tough. Resilient leaders think about continuous improvement as well as competitive advantage in everything they do. We also suggested reinforcing the five core competency behaviors all team members should have during mid-year progress check ins and end-of- year performance reviews. Let's agree that attaining our objectives is a balance of "did you get it done" and "how did you get the team engaged in getting it done".

I'd like to share a couple of items that influenced me and continue to play a role in my journey and roadmap. You can reflect on what influences you in your journey to succeed and how it supports your leadership mindset.

Parental Role Models

As far back as I can recall, I've had a competitive mindset. It likely began with the work ethic I observed in my parents as a first-generation child of Hungarian immigrants. The pride taken in their heritage, their work ethic, how they embraced very difficult challenges, and reaching the "American Dream" resonates with me to this day.

That being said, I also celebrate others' successes. Admiring those who are more successful than me, analyzing what they did to succeed, and figuring out how to join them in being successful has benefitted me as well. By seeing examples of honesty, kindness, hard work, responsibility, and respect for others, you cannot help but think it is the right thing to do.

Parental role modeling means acting the way you want your child to behave and perform. The same examples apply to leading teams through what seems like insurmountable challenges where many people stop, freeze, and look for someone else to take the lead. Take the opportunity to apply the right behaviors in attaining objectives that seem too extreme for some. Having the discipline to overcome challenges by using the right behaviors begins with how we see our parents, role models, and managers lead, follow, and guide the way.

Rhinoceros Success

Many years ago, I read an article about the book Rhinoceros Success by Scott Alexander, (1980)[2]. Intrigued, I bought the book and have been influenced by it ever since. It's a great motivational book that inspires you to charge at your problems, take on obstacles, and drop the fear of the unknown. Among key takeaways from the book are:

- There are two kinds of people in the world—cows and rhinos, and you get to choose which one you want to be.

- *"Charge with rhinos, fly with eagles, run with cheetahs, and eat with lions. Don't hang around with cows or sheep."*
- Believing and succeeding turns unsurmountable adversity into success on your own terms.
- Take rhinoceros training, determination, and thick skin to charge persistently toward your own goals.
- Being a rhino means not to slip back into the pasture with the cud-chewing cows awaiting their slaughter.
- Use your rhino imagination and creativity to solve every problem.
- Obstacles are merely hurdles to break through, not roadblocks that immobilize you.
- Be full of energy every morning, so write your big picture goal and get moving.
- Success happens one step at a time, whether the goal is large or small.

You can see how this benefits you and your team in taking on obstacles, charging through them in a persistent manner, and solving any other obstacles throughout the course of your journey. In addition, Scott Alexander reminds his audience to take a few breaks during the year and relax in the mudhole with your family. Balance work and family. You can combine the two by involving family in your work. Rhinos do not do work that is boring—they do work that is seen as a hobby. Rhinos know loving what you do makes you successful. There is no better way to love the work that you do than by involving those you love in your work! Rhinos love problems because it means that they are making progress. If you don't have problems, you are not taking action on your goals. Buy the book and decide today to become a rhino and make the rest of your life the best of your life!

Celebrate success with your team and know when and how to take effective breaks from everything that entails building and maintaining operational resilience.

Hate to Lose Mindset

Let's compare the operational resilience mindset to that of a competitive athlete. World class athletes are resilient. There is a difference in the psychology of performance when it comes to having to win or hating to lose. Everyone likes to win, but many world-class athletes have stated that hating to lose is what motivated them. Muhammad Ali, Jimmy Connors, Michael Phelps, and Kobe Bryant are a few who hated losing so much, they made extreme personal sacrifices to avoid losing. It drove their competitive performance. They spent much more time than their competitors did in training and practicing. They convinced themselves they needed to outwork anyone else they competed against. They kept trying as long as there was even a remote chance they might lose. Even when a loss was unavoidable, they kept working and trying their best until it was over.

Let's agree that being competitive has both positive and negative implications. You need to motivate without being overbearing. A toxic response to hating to lose by taking shortcuts or cheating in some way should be avoided. Competitive leaders can drive their teams to be resilient in multiple ways. We've outlined a few suggestions for you as a starting point in this book. Surrounding yourself with competitive teammates who have a similar mindset to you can help you accomplish great things.

When I trained and tested for my first-degree black belt, I used the hate to lose mindset as a motivation and it led to success. The same training and performance went into every additional martial arts black belt test up to and including my fifth-degree black belt test which led into my induction into The World Martial Arts Hall of Fame.

In corporate cardio challenges, I tracked the performance of those who were in the top tier with me. I had to work harder than them so I would not lose, which led to wins in every one of the individual and team cardio challenges I entered. In addition, the world record I set for marine corps style pushups was attained since I could not see myself losing that goal. Likewise, I successfully led teams in responding to crises throughout the years as a loss was unacceptable. I knew it and my management knew it. All our team members knew it. Our teams outperformed other companies when facing hurricanes, earthquakes, strikes, political insurrections, infectious disease, and human element crises in every region and country. Regardless of the differences in languages, cultures, and time zones, we delivered excellence in executing our objectives. We could not lose our goal of ensuring our associates were safe and healthy, our facilities remained intact, and our business operations remained resilient. Our teams' hating to lose mentality promoted innovation, passion, new ideas, continuous improvement, competitive advantage, and success.

You can make your own decision as to whether hating to lose or having to win is a motivator for your organization and the teams you lead. That being said, it may be better to avoid the win-loss discussion altogether and simply focus on executing your objectives. Keep in mind that every athlete and leader who wants to be elite hates losing and also loves the feeling of when they or their teams win. Hating to lose and wanting to win are both important. What separates many of us is how we use mental skills to manage our goals and motivations. This topic is included under objectives in the book since it is a great example of the combined impact of personal and business resilience advice. To recap, the best approach to excellence in operational resilience is to lead, follow, and guide the way.

How to Lead, Follow, and Guide the Way

Your organization's mission statement provides for decision making and direction and unifies all associates toward a common long-term goal. Your team's operational resilience objectives should remain aligned with the mission statement. The objective setting and management process helps maintain focus on successful resilient deployment activities.

o **Identify and address potential obstacles in meeting objectives.** Ensure all of your teams understand the objectives they are asked to support along with the metrics used to help keep track of progress throughout the year. Look for their commitment to their completion in their actions towards attaining desired results. Reach out to their direct managers and operational leadership prior to setting the objectives to ensure you have their support.

o **Follow a common objective setting and management process across your organization.** Remain aligned with your organization's annual objective setting and monitoring process. It's much easier to have participation in a process that's already understood. Keep objectives SMART. Include monthly, mid-year, and annual progress check-ins. Global and regional leaders have greater responsibility and accountability, so their objectives should be more detailed than those for operational team members. All objectives should be aligned with the mission statement.

o **Identify any issues with time commitments to attain the aligned objectives.** Encourage all team members to track their objective related time commitments through their blocks of work summary. Consider a monthly summary that includes alignment meetings, training, documentation, and process improvement activities. Understand the importance of the time required in planning for and responding to incidents, crises, and business continuity events. If time commitments become a challenge, get support from operational leadership immediately.

o **Monitor your teams' performance, providing individual and team support needed to obstacles presented.** Use a common method to engage all team members in reporting any issues they encounter in reaching their objectives. Maintain consistent dialogue with their direct managers and quarterly reviews with the operational teams. Make the quarterly reviews a formal report by all team members. Include both primary and alternate team members. In addition to focusing on objectives, keep track of the behaviors that support their successful accomplishment.

o **Inspire your team through personal resilience strategies that benefit them and the entire organization.** Use your own personal resilience background and experience to help inspire and lead your teams. The life lessons you have learned help you prepare for issues your teams are facing. Remember that a resilient organization makes use of the personal resilience capabilities of their leaders.

How to Lead

Align your operational resilience objective process with your organization's annual objective setting and management process. Prepare objectives and metrics that tie back to your project plan through your resilient deployment process. Consider what you see as time constraints of your team members when setting the objectives, goals, strategies, and measures.

How to Follow

Gain feedback from all key stakeholders prior to formalizing the annual objective process. Follow guidance from human resources and operational leadership in developing an approved common objective.

How to Guide the Way

- Monitor any obstacles in reaching your goals through weekly, monthly, and quarterly meetings with your teams.
- Immediately address any issues you observe with time commitments with managers and operational leadership.
- Modify objectives if needed as long as they remain aligned with the organization's mission.
- Reflect on your own personal resilience background and how it can support your team.
- Share motivational examples experienced by your teams.
- Support behaviors that help promote progress and encourage correcting behaviors that detract from it.

Notes

1 Jackie Wiles, '9 Steps to Successful Functional Strategic Planning', Gartner, 2023, https://www.gartner.com/smarterwithgartner/9-steps-successful-functional-strategic-planning
2 Scott Alexander, *Rhinoceros Success: the Secret to Charging Full Speed Toward Every Opportunity*, Ramsey Press, 2003.

Chapter VII

Maturity Model

As you are completing the resilient deployment process, focus on how well your teams execute their current-year objectives. Track objectives monthly in your scorecard and share the results with regional teams and operational leadership. This allows you time to make corrections to issues that can stall your progress throughout the year. Consider surveying all your regional facility contacts toward the end of the year to receive feedback on their progress to promote continuous improvement. Using that survey, establish a resilient maturity model which is a tool you can develop and use to track progress on your operational resilience objectives and your capability for continuous improvement. This maturity model helps determine levels of effectiveness and identify what items need attention to improve maturity. Your maturity model will not fix inefficiencies. Instead, it can identify actions needed to operate at an attainable standard. If the maturity model is well defined with attainable objectives, it can help reveal the actions needed to reach the next level of maturity.

In this chapter, we will provide advice on how to effectively construct and maximize the value of a maturity model to improve capabilities for operational resilience.

- Selecting Maturity Components
- Defining Maturity Levels
- Determining "Good," "Better," and "Best"
- Setting Appropriate Goals

Selecting Maturity Components

Every item we have defined as being part of our toolbox, along with our scorecard and our project plan, helps support operational resilience. You need to evaluate current and evolving international standards, regulations, and technology as you progress through resilient deployment. When I

DOI: 10.4324/9781003438700-7

developed the roadmap for Goodyear's business continuity policy, charter, and global structure over two decades ago, I knew that aligning with an established and respected framework would provide my teams with a great starting point. Goodyear has successfully followed and built its operational resilience process around the Professional Practices for Business Continuity Management[1] as published and maintained by Disaster Recovery Institute (DRI) International[2].

The Professional Practices are a body of knowledge designed to assist in the development, implementation, testing and maintenance of a Business Continuity Program (BCP). It is a management process that supports operational resilience quite well. The Professional Practices continue to be updated and adapted to changing standards and regulations and provide the basis for Goodyear's Maturity of Excellence internal benchmarking and process improvement model.

We will review how each of the Professional Practices support and promote our goal to maintain excellence in operational resilience. You can either gain support for or improve your operational resilience process as outlined through the objectives and benefits for each of the Professional Practices below. We will develop maturity levels for each of the Professional Practices supporting operational resilience next.

Program Management

Objectives – Establish the need for a BCP with leadership support and funding. Introduce the key components of your toolbox such as program management, risk awareness, BIA, business impacts of critical functions and processes, recovery strategies, training and awareness, and exercise testing. Align the program objectives to those of the organization's mission. Implement the BCP throughout the organization.

Operational Resilience Benefits – Relevant business, legal, regulatory, and contractual requirements are reviewed with recommendations on conformity. Conflicts in governance policies, procedures, and requirements are revealed to correct any gaps and maintain effectiveness. Awareness is increased on the importance of leadership's role, accountability, liability, and evaluating the potential impact of risks.

A charter for the program is developed and tied to the organization's mission. Budgets, resources, program governance, structure, and oversight are acquired. The scope, responsibility, and accountability for every key role is tied to the process are documented and funded.

A steering committee is created and aligned with organizational policies. Teams are created to support the implementation of the business continuity activities outlined in all the adopted Professional Practices. Documentation for tracking overall effectiveness of the program is created. A schedule to report on the status of the BCP is in place. Recommendations for process improvements are provided. Regulations and industry standards are monitored to ensure the BCP delivers value consistent with current best practices.

Risk Assessment

Objectives – Identify significant risks affecting your organization. Determine the most effective methods to engage resources in appropriate risk management methods.

Operational Resilience Benefits – A single, consolidated method to assess risks and actual incidents affecting the organization is in place. A common way to measure the probability and impact of the risks and effectiveness of any existing controls exists. All applicable natural, human (people), and technological risks are considered. Changes that benefit the organization by reducing the impact of risks are considered, which include improvements to physical protection, security and access controls, cyber security and IT systems, policies, procedures, communication, and training. A consolidated risk analysis is presented to operational leadership, including findings and recommendations for improvement. Leadership feedback is documented, evaluated and implemented.

BIA

Objectives – Identify and prioritize the organization's processes, functions, and dependencies to determine the greatest impacts if a disruption should occur. Include current gaps between requirements and capabilities and communicate them to operational leadership and other key stakeholders.

Operational Resilience Benefits – A single BIA process is in place. Leadership support is obtained for the tools used to gather information. The data is analyzed and prioritized in a uniform way. All the dependencies between the business processes are consolidated. The priorities for recovery efforts are prepared and presented to operational leadership. The overall organizational impact analysis, including financial, regulatory, customer, contractual, operational, and reputational impacts, is completed. New regulations are evaluated and integrated into the BIA process. An acceptable timeframe for recovery is documented and shared with key stakeholders.

Business Continuity Strategies

Objective – Select strategies to reduce gaps identified during the risk assessment and BIA.

Operational Resilience Benefits – The strategies for meeting recovery time and point objectives are identified and possible business continuity strategies are also considered. These strategies include the use of multi-usage spaces, as well as internal and external alternate sites. In our example detailed in Chapter 5, the global manufacturer's regions are considering various manufacturing and distribution alternate strategies, including making onsite repairs, shifting production elsewhere, improving labor productivity, and finding creative ways to meet customer needs. Vital records, such as financial, regulatory, contracts and insurance coverages, are under review. Supply chain impacts are being considered for raw materials and finished goods.

Incident Preparedness and Response

Objectives – Understand the types of incidents and potential impacts the organization may experience. Comply with related regulatory requirements. Implement an incident command system that includes internal and external resources.

Operational Resilience Benefits – Human, natural, and technological threats have been identified. The probabilities of threats, the magnitude of impacts, organizational vulnerabilities, prevention measures, and mitigation strategies are all under review. All applicable regulations have been identified and complied with. Documented plans are in place that support appropriate life safety and property protection measures, and external response times and support are taken into consideration. A resource assessment to provide an accurate inventory is conducted. Communication strategies are considered. Emergency command and operations are in place to maximize the effectiveness of internal and external supporting roles. Documents are shared with internal and external teams, agencies, and resources. Formal approval of plans and procedures has been obtained.

Plan Development and Implementation

Objectives – Document the plans the organization will use during incidents. Define the method of evaluating the plans to ensure they provide for the organization's continued operation.

Operational Resilience Benefits – Recovery strategies are part of operational planning. The plan documents the required resources, people, facilities, and technology. Regional roles, structures, and responsibilities are included. Business continuity and crisis management planning and programs are in place. Internal and external notification and communication strategies are documented. Operational recovery plans include team members' information, tools, resources, hardware, and software support. Infrastructure and information security is included in planning. The plan is prepared, reviewed, and approved by appropriate operational leadership. Copies are distributed to interested parties.

Awareness and Training Programs

Objectives – Establish and maintain training and awareness across the organization in order to respond to and effectively manage disruptive events.

Operational Resilience Benefits – An awareness and training program is developed, approved, and implemented across all business operations. It is aligned with existing organizational policies and procedures. Those receiving the training are made aware of its purpose and benefits. Relevant incident, business continuity, and crisis management team members are included. The appropriate onsite and external incident activities are included (e.g., shelter in place, evacuate, etc.). The training materials include courseware, websites, social media tools, apps, conferences, and publications. The effectiveness of the program is monitored and evaluated. Activities that promote continuous improvement to meet evolving organizational needs are included. Awareness programs include the organization's new hires as part of onboarding.

Business Continuity Plan Exercise, Test, Assessment, and Maintenance

Objectives – Establish an exercise, test, assessment, and maintenance program to improve the state of readiness across all operations.

Operational Resilience Benefits – Documented operational resilience planning is tested and maintained current. Walk throughs, tabletops, and notification programs are included. Internal and external interdependencies are exercised and tested. All appropriate team members are included. The top operational risks are a basis for the testing. They are tested on at least an annual basis or more frequently if critical processes warrant it. The testing includes identifying objectives, participants, criteria, and expected outcomes. All action items from the testing are monitored for completion. Plans are updated and maintained as needed. As a result of successful training, audits of your resilience program reveal minimal findings. The business continuity planning testing conducted by global and regional teams cascades to all facilities and critical locations.

Crisis Communications

Objectives – Create and maintain an organizational crisis communications plan. Ensure the plan includes both internal and external stakeholders.

Operational Resilience Benefits – Crisis communications plans are aligned with the relevant operational priority risks. The crisis communications team is structured. Primary locations for the team's operation are in place. The intended audiences for the crisis communications messages are pre-defined and modified as necessary. An approval plan for distributing communications is in place. The method for crisis communications includes appropriate incident notification, emails, conference calls, intranet systems, press conferences, and media sources. Members of the crisis communications team are trained in their roles and responsibilities. Exercises and tests are completed. Corrective actions are documented and verified as complete for any gaps identified through tests. The crisis communications plans are tested annually at a minimum or more frequently if needed.

Coordinating with External Agencies and Resources

Objectives – Establish policies and procedures to coordinate resources for incident preparedness and response. Identify requirements for compliance with agencies having jurisdiction and applicable public entities and private resources.

Operational Resilience Benefits – Agencies having jurisdiction with operational facilities are identified, along with their requirements for reporting and coordinating responses to relevant incidents. First responder notification and mandatory reporting of hazmat, injuries, and other incidents are understood. First responders are invited to tour facilities and asked to provide recommendations on improvements to incident response plans. Exercises and training drills with external agencies are conducted to increase awareness, promote compliance with regulations, and improve response capabilities.

Defining Maturity Levels

Maturity is defined by Merriam Webster as the quality or state of being mature, having attained a full or desired state[3]. Maturity models help define the capability of your organization to improve from a given state to a desired state. They help support continuous improvement and are linked to your operational resilience project planning. Our maturity model will consider qualitative information based on the Professional Practices. The path of our resilience process ranges from emerging to being well integrated and fully mature across our operations.

Let's agree on the use of five levels or stages in measuring our maturity. A five-point scale should be used because it is a universal method of evaluating data, and the format aligns with many external benchmarking levels. People are familiar with it, and it provides a couple of levels above and below a neutral or mid-point, and it is not overly complicated.

Let's define the five levels of our maturity model and summarize them in Table 7.1. Afterwards, we'll define what is needed to attain the levels of maturity for each Professional Practice.

Emerging – Maturity Level 1

Maturity Level 1 is also known as being an **ad hoc** stage of maturity. At Maturity Level 1, an organization has an inconsistent, basic, and informal approach to risk and resilience management, most likely at a site (versus regional or global) level. The organization does not fully understand risks and exposures and does not have appropriate resource allocation. No one is responsible for monitoring key components of a resilient deployment process. They have devoted minimal education around the tools, techniques,

Table 7.1 Business continuity maturity levels

Business Continuity Maturity Level of Excellence

Maturity Level	Description
Emerging (1)	Business continuity process does not exist or is ineffective.
Reactive (2)	Business continuity process exists, but it is underdeveloped or not integrated. Performance is maintained without appreciable improvements.
Compliant (3)	Business continuity process elements exist. Performance is improving slowly.
Proactive (4)	Superior business continuity process is in place with continuous performance improvement.
Integrated (5)	Best in class fully integrated business continuity process exists with evidence of top performance and use of predictive indicators!

and solutions to issues that will be encountered. Other terms that can be referenced for Maturity Level 1 include foundational, ad hoc, informal, and initial.

Reactive – Maturity Level 2

Maturity Level 2 can be considered a **repeatable** stage of maturity. At this level, an organization has more consistency in their approach to responding to disruptive events. Certain teams and departments focus on risk and resilience, but they are fragmented and there is no overall coordination. Processes and programs are not integrated. They follow documented plans without a full understanding of their meaning. Standardization is inconsistent. Activities are executed manually, and the level of effectiveness is not where it needs to be. Other terms that can be referenced for Maturity Level 2 include visible, fragmented, reactive, repeatable, and tracked.

Compliant – Maturity Level 3

Maturity Level 3 can be called a **defined** stage of maturity. The elements of a solid resilience plan exist. The process is gaining acceptance and moving slowly ahead. Some areas are managed well at a regional level, but the plan does not cascade to all locations and facilities. There is a lack of consistent reporting. Oversight, responsibility, and accountability throughout the organization are beginning to appear. The entire program has more visibility with greater associate awareness. Audits are underway and teams interact with one another. Skills and knowledge of team members are increasing to a common level across the operations. Other terms to reference for Maturity Level 3 include defined, predictable and tactical.

Proactive – Maturity Level 4

Maturity Level 4 is a **strategic** stage of maturity. Greater control and monitoring of all resilient deployment activities are evident. All qualitative and quantitative objectives are clearly defined and understood. Continuous improvement feedback across the organization is received. Metrics are aligned with the organization's mission. Assessments are accurately completed, and audits result in minimal negative findings. However, not all systems, processes, and programs are fully integrated. Other terms to consider for Maturity Level 4 include managed, resilient, strategic and controlled.

Integrated – Maturity Level 5

Maturity Level 5 can be considered **sustainable**. Frameworks supporting resilience are embedded across all operations and locations in a standardized manner. A dashboard provides for oversight of all plans and incident management. The focus is on improving the performance of all processes. New tools and techniques are consistently evaluated and introduced. The causes of all gaps and flaws are found and remediated. Everything is well integrated. Objectives improve performance. All regions are equally skilled at employing resilience tools and techniques. All teams have a complete understanding of the benefits of organizational resilience and there is minimal resistance to time commitments. Risk management and insurance coverage is integrated into the process. Common terms to consider for Maturity Level 5 include sustainable, optimized, and agile.

Let us review how a Maturity of Excellence survey referencing the Professional Practices can be of benefit in attaining excellence in operational resilience. The survey is intended to be completed by each location or facility and references the BCP. We will take each of the ten Professional Practices as defined in Tables 7.2 through 7.11 and clearly describe what it takes to evolve from Emerging (Level 1) to being fully Integrated (Level 5) across all operations throughout your organization. As you progress in maturity from Level 1 to Level 5, the elements include successfully maintaining those from all previous levels.

Program Management

Table 7.2 Program management maturity level survey

Program Management Maturity Level Survey	
Maturity Level	Elements
Emerging (1)	A BCP coordinator and BCP teams are in place: A BCP coordinator and committee is appointed and authorized to develop, implement, administer, evaluate, and maintain the local BCP. Global policy compliance can be demonstrated.
Reactive (2)	BCP ongoing sustainability is established: BCP documents are reviewed annually and approved by facility leadership. A current BCP project plan aligned with the region is being implemented.
Compliant (3)	BCP "project management" is documented: There is a structured process for developing the BCP in place with tracking of performance vs. agreed upon objectives, schedules, and milestones. The BCP coordinator is identified on the facility organizational chart with a succession plan in place to ensure the role is backfilled when needed.

(Continued)

Table 7.2 (Continued)

Program Management Maturity Level Survey

Maturity Level	Elements
Proactive (4)	BCP project initiation findings and lessons learned are shared locally and regionally (if applicable) including with all regions that can benefit by referencing them. BCP proactively addresses critical business aspects: Includes proactive planning of business process components (e.g., protection of resources, alternative materials, technology, and processes).
Integrated (5)	BCP reactively addresses critical business aspects: Includes incident response plans or emergency response plans, crisis management plans, and all other reactive process components. BCP is managed through a formal team approach: Responsibilities for planning, response, recovery, and testing are documented and assigned to team members as part of their BCP individual personal objectives with documented training strategies in place. BCP audit results clearly indicate complete alignment between self-assessments of program management and those conducted by external regulators or internal audit.

Risk Assessment

Table 7.3 Risk analysis maturity level survey

Risk Assessment Maturity Level Survey

Maturity Level	Elements
Emerging (1)	Risk assessment is documented: Latest annual risk assessment is completed and is part of the annual BIA/risk assessment. Risk evaluations are done at facilities and can include loss control reports; risk maps; risk evaluation by insurers; annual BIA/risk assessment.
Reactive (2)	All appropriate risks are considered: Risk assessment includes natural (e.g., fire, flooding, disease), human (e.g., infectious disease, bomb threats, sabotage), and technological types (e.g., IT system downtime, resource and material shortages, customer service, equipment failure), including those indirectly impacting site or function (e.g., incidents at a supplier's or service provider's site or function).

(Continued)

Table 7.3 (Continued)

Risk Assessment Maturity Level Survey

Maturity Level	Elements
Compliant (3)	Risk resilience (evaluation, acceptance, avoidance, transfer) actions are discussed and understood with the leadership. If risks are accepted (no mitigation action planned), the decision is documented. Mitigation or transfer measures are identified and introduced in a documented action plan that includes responsibilities, resource requirements, and milestones.
Proactive (4)	Costs and benefits are a decision criterion for mitigation measures: Documentation is available regarding costs justifying a measure taking into account the risk.
Integrated (5)	Residual risks are considered: Risks which remain after risk avoidance efforts are identified, quantified, and included again in the risk assessment. Risk assessment findings and lessons learned are shared locally and regionally (if applicable). BCP audit results clearly indicate complete alignment between self-assessments of risk assessments and those conducted by external regulators or internal audit. Risk transfer coverage is evaluated as part of the overall strategy.

BIA

Table 7.4 BIA Maturity level survey

BIA Maturity Level Survey

Maturity Level	Elements
Emerging (1)	A process for overall BCP strategic analysis is established with senior management: Include a review of options relating to prevention, mitigation, resource management, mutual aid, communications and warning, and operational procedures. Strategies are based upon reducing deficiencies as identified in the risk assessment and BIA.
Reactive (2)	BCP strategic analysis is implemented: Include system and associate offsite or work remote program. Contracts are signed (if applicable), strategies are tested on a regional level via tabletop exercise.
Compliant (3)	Strategies remain current (valid, kept up to date): Strategies are updated and adjusted based upon the most recent data from vendors or other regions, post-incident data, lessons learned, etc. Strategies are aligned with global sourcing and business objectives. Options may include transfer, mitigation, or acceptance of the risks.

(Continued)

Table 7.4 (Continued)

BIA Maturity Level Survey	
Maturity Level	Elements
Proactive (4)	BCP alternate strategy findings and lessons learned are shared locally. New regulations are evaluated and integrated into the BIA process.
Integrated (5)	BCP alternate strategy findings and lessons learned are shared locally and regionally (if applicable): Share with all regions what you discovered in your strategy planning and use lessons learned to help all regions. BCP audit results clearly indicate complete alignment between self-assessments of business continuity strategies and those conducted by external regulators or internal audit.

Business Continuity Strategies

Table 7.5 Business continuity strategies maturity level survey

Business Continuity Strategies Maturity Level Survey	
Maturity Level	Elements
Emerging (1)	A process for overall BCP strategic analysis is established with senior management: Include a review of options relating to prevention, mitigation, resource management, mutual aid, communications and warning, and operational procedures. Strategies are based upon reducing deficiencies as identified in the risk assessment and BIA.
Reactive (2)	BCP strategic analysis is implemented: Include system and associate offsite or work remote program. Contracts are signed (if applicable), strategies are tested on a regional level via tabletop exercise.
Compliant (3)	Strategies remain current (valid, kept up to date): Strategies are updated and adjusted based upon updated data from vendors or other regions, post incident data, lessons learned, etc. Strategies are aligned with global sourcing and business objectives. Option may include transfer, mitigation, or acceptance of the risks.
Proactive (4)	BCP alternate strategy findings and lessons learned are shared locally.
Integrated (5)	BCP alternate strategy findings and lessons learned are shared locally and regionally (if applicable): Share with all regions what you discovered in your strategy planning and use lessons learned to help all regions. BCP audit results clearly indicate complete alignment between self-assessments of business continuity strategies and those conducted by external regulators or internal audit.

Incident Preparedness and Response

Table 7.6 Incident preparedness and response maturity level survey

Incident Preparedness and Response Maturity Level Survey

Maturity Level	Elements
Emerging (1)	Incident response plan: A plan on the immediate response to human, natural, technological incidents (with link to local risks/threats) exists. The plan is updated annually and identifies actions to be taken to protect people, property, operations, the environment and to provide stabilization. Incident notification: An effective incident notification and reporting process following the regional requirements is in place. Responsible people are trained on their roles for carrying out specific actions during incidents.
Reactive (2)	Incident management and general awareness: All associates are trained and aware of their role that they will have during incidents to direct, control, coordinate, and recover during incidents (e.g., what to do if an incident is detected, how to evacuate, how to support incident response, how to inform emergency response providers, how to deal with external inquiries).
Compliant (3)	Emergency Operations Centers (EOCs) are established: Include a primary and alternate EOC capable of managing response, continuity, and recovery operations.
Proactive (4)	Shut down of equipment: Plans describe how to safely and orderly shutdown and de-energize equipment in case of an emergency. Critical security and safety plans: Plans describe how to secure site (avoid entry of non-authorized persons in case of an emergency) and how to secure people (including visitor, contractor). Crisis management process: Local crisis management team members are nominated and informed on roles. The meeting process (scope, what triggers meeting, where to meet, team duty) is defined.
Integrated (5)	Internal responder: Potential internal responders (e.g., first aiders, fire brigade, medical) or functions (i.e., HR, security, facilities, communication, legal) and their contact information and the contact process are defined. They are effectively trained according to local legal or regulatory requirements. External emergency service: Plans contain all external emergency service provider contact information and how the contact process should work (who calls and when). Examples include police, fire, ambulance, insurance company, equipment service contractors, and other recovery support (e.g., cleaning, re-building, engineering). Emergency response findings and lessons learned are shared locally and regionally (if applicable): Share with all regions what you discovered in your planning and use lessons learned to help all regions. BCP audit results clearly indicate complete alignment between self-assessments of incident response and those conducted by external regulators or internal auditors.

Plan Development and Implementation

Table 7.7 Plan development and implementation maturity level survey

Plan Development and Implementation Maturity Level Survey	
Maturity Level	Elements
Emerging (1)	Business continuity plans include associates/contractors of important (time-critical) business processes and contact information: Emergency contact phone numbers identified.
Reactive (2)	Business continuity plans include vendors and customers (external and internal) and contact information: Emergency contact phone numbers identified.
Compliant (3)	Business continuity plans include IT backup and recovery plans identified: IT has consulted with the business and provided a summary of critical IT requirements.
Proactive (4)	Business continuity plans include equipment identified: Global engineering (or appropriate group) has consulted with the business and provided a summary of critical equipment requirements.
	Business continuity plans include alternate site or offsite work strategies: All appropriate team members are aware of their role and the process to work off-site if needed.
	Business continuity plans include key business records identified: Key business records (data, paper) and how to protect them identified (back-up, storage etc.).
	Business continuity plans clearly identify all downstream processes for relevant incidents with appropriate actions to be promptly taken.
Integrated (5)	Business continuity plans are reviewed and approved annually by site management: Plans are updated minimally annually or when improvement items become known or are communicated by a region, a function, or other sites.
	Business continuity plan findings and lessons learned are shared locally and regionally (if applicable): Share with all regions what you discovered in your plans and use lessons learned to help all regions.
	BCP audit results clearly indicate complete alignment between self-assessments of plan development and implementation and those conducted by external regulators or internal audit.

Awareness and Training Programs

Table 7.8 Awareness and training programs maturity level survey

Awareness and Training Programs Maturity Level Survey	
Maturity Level	Elements
Emerging (1)	Awareness and training programs are documented and maintained. Specific regulatory training needs and content are defined and executed: Requirements by specific job function comply with all local and legal requirements (e.g. fire brigades, medical staff).
Reactive (2)	A new hire orientation program includes basic business continuity overview: All new associates are trained on business continuity principles (including role expectations, incident notification, behavior in case of an incident, how can they support business continuity efforts). Emergency (incident) response is included in a formal training process: All associates in fire brigades, first aiders, security, etc., are trained on the emergency response process and their duties.
Compliant (3)	Crisis management is included in a formal training process: All associates with roles in crisis notification and actions to be taken are trained in the process and their duties. Incident classification and notification is included in a formal training process: All associates with roles in the incident classification and notification process and actions to be taken are trained in the process and their duties.
Proactive (4)	External partners are included in a formal training process: Key suppliers, contractors, partners, customers, etc., are trained on specific requirements when potentially interfering with business continuity performance. A general awareness program for all associates exists: Provide incident awareness and method of notification, including evacuation, de-energization of equipment, and other immediate actions to take).
Integrated (5)	Documents are translated as needed (if applicable): If needed, some programs are translated for native speakers. Findings and lessons learned are shared locally and regionally (if applicable): This includes lessons learned from actual incidents and from the training program overall (actual incidents, effective training techniques and programs, etc.) to help all regions. BCP audit results clearly indicate complete alignment between self-assessments of awareness and training programs and those conducted by external regulators or internal audit).

Business Continuity Plan Exercise Assessment and Maintenance

Table 7.9 Business continuity plan, exercise, assessment and maintenance maturity level survey

Business Continuity Plan Exercise, Assessment and Maintenance Maturity Level Survey	
Maturity Level	Elements
Emerging (1)	Testing (exercise) program: A formal testing program exists which defines which plans are tested when and how. Program is documented (i.e., Word, PowerPoint, Outlook). Testing format can include tabletop exercises, IT disaster recovery exercises, evacuation or shelter drills, and simulations. Testing will meet regulatory requirements (if applicable).
Reactive (2)	Testing frequency: All plans are tested on a schedule to meet internal and regulatory requirements. When not specified, the minimum frequency for testing is annually, when significant business or associate related changes occur. Debriefing: A debriefing with all test participants after a test is always done (for reviewing performance and identifying any plan improvement items).
Compliant (3)	Continuous improvement: A corrective action plan (including responsibilities and milestones) exists for all significant improvement items and is communicated to all test participants (no formal plan is needed for immediate and easy fixes). Improvement action is tracked until regional leadership has documented satisfaction with action taken.
Proactive (4)	Incident notification: Business continuity incidents (minor and major) are always notified as per regional requirements to local/regional stakeholder.
Integrated (5)	Incident investigation: All business continuity incidents are investigated and the incident root cause is used for defining corrective action. Findings and lessons learned are shared locally and regionally (if applicable): This includes lessons learned from actual incidents and from the testing program overall (actual incidents, effective training techniques and programs, etc.) to help all regions. BCP audit results clearly indicate complete alignment between self-assessments of business continuity plan exercise, assessment and maintenance, and those conducted by external regulators or internal audit.

Crisis Communications

Table 7.10 Crisis communications maturity level survey

Crisis Communications Maturity Level Survey	
Maturity Level	*Elements*
Emerging (1)	The communication department is a member of the appropriate local business continuity teams that manage incidents and crises: They can include facility or local teams and business unit teams.
Reactive (2)	Crisis communications plans are developed: They are flexible to include potential incident scenarios, severity levels, and the communication approach (templates).
Compliant (3)	Plans consider external and internal audiences: Include methods of delivering messages to each audience to ensure consistent and effective communication.
Proactive (4)	The communication process demonstrates an ability to immediately approve internal and external messages in support of the business continuity team due to timeliness required in response to social media.
Integrated (5)	Media training: An evaluation is conducted and all persons who could potentially talk with external partners (including the media) during an incident are trained as required. Findings and lessons learned are shared locally and regionally (if applicable): Share with all regions what you discovered in lessons learned and from the communications program overall (actual incidents, effective training techniques and programs, etc.) to help all regions. BCP audit results clearly indicate complete alignment between self-assessments of crisis communications and those conducted by external regulators or internal audit).

Coordination with External Agencies

Table 7.11 Coordination with external agencies maturity level survey

Coordination with External Agencies Maturity Level Survey	
Maturity Level	*Elements*
Emerging (1)	Applicable public plans and contacts are fully integrated and referenced in business continuity internal plans: Business process related local public authorities and partners are identified. Include updated emergency contact information as part of the plans.
Reactive (2)	Documentation of coordination with public authorities is maintained: Ensure appropriate public authorities are included in reviewing plans, receiving training, and being aware of mutual aid strategies as needed. An annual assessment of which external agencies are most critical is conducted.

(Continued)

Table 7.11 (Continued)

Coordination with External Agencies Maturity Level Survey

Maturity Level	Elements
Compliant (3)	Approved process of sharing information is established: The relevant details have been verified with the legal and communications departments (what may be disclosed and how). Confidential and personal information is sufficiently protected.
Proactive (4)	Notification channels with public authorities are established: A process has been reviewed and is documented on how notification between parties will occur in case of an upcoming incident in compliance with local regulations.
	Local and regional emergency plans are shared with public authorities.
Integrated (5)	Facility awareness training is conducted: Public authorities are trained in facility specific business continuity plans and processes per mutually agreeable schedules and procedures.
	Findings and lessons learned are shared locally and regionally (if applicable).
	BCP audit results clearly indicate complete alignment between self-assessments of coordination with external agencies and those conducted by external regulators or internal audit).

Determining "Good," "Better," and "Best"

We analyzed each of the Professional Practices and clearly defined activities to help track your progress evolving from Emerging (Level 1) to being fully Integrated (Level 5). What is your next step? Integrate the maturity model into your resilient deployment process. Start by having your regional leaders identify who will be receiving the maturity survey at each of your major facilities. They will be the business continuity contact at each site. Using our global manufacturer example, we will have each of the four regional business continuity leaders send each site contact an advance explanation of the survey. Set up regional meetings to review the survey and answer any of their questions. You are asking for an accurate assessment of how your activities support operational resilience. Each regional facility contact should be encouraged to have a cross functional team join them in completing the survey. Once the surveys are returned, analyze each one of the Professional Practices by region and globally. The initial survey provides a baseline of how your team members are making progress towards the objectives and goals you have established. It also provides valuable

Table 7.12 Maturity model survey

Maturity of Excellence Baseline Survey Results

Professional Practice	Region A Average	Region B Average	Region C Average	Region D Average	Global Average
(1)	2.44	2.08	2.60	2.88	**2.50**
(2)	3.10	2.85	2.99	3.22	**3.04**
(3)	2.86	2.60	2.53	2.77	**2.69**
(4)	2.29	2.33	2.40	2.45	**2.37**
(5)	3.11	3.20	2.89	3.33	**3.13**
(6)	2.86	2.90	2.81	2.92	**2.87**
(7)	2.71	2.55	2.67	2.90	**2.71**
(8)	2.43	2.33	2.51	2.44	**2.43**
(9)	3.12	2.67	2.65	2.85	**2.82**
(10)	2.44	2.10	2.35	2.73	**2.40**
Average (1-10)	**2.74**	**2.56**	**2.64**	**2.85**	**2.70**

Key Takeaways:

1. All four of the regions have similar average maturity levels.
2. Incident preparedness and response is a strength across all operations.
3. Coordination with external agencies is the greatest opportunity for improvement.
4. The overall global maturity level is Reactive, below a Compliant level.

feedback on how their blocks of work are committed to operational resilience. Let us create an example of results of a baseline maturity survey completed by our global manufacturer with four business units as seen in Table 7.12.

The baseline maturity scores provide a great starting point to determine what can be considered good, better, and best. Based on the regional and global survey feedback, we can leverage the results and tie them to our resilient deployment process to improve operational resilience. As our next step, let us review a suggestion for a continuous improvement plan that's part of our journey and that ties to effective project planning.

Setting Appropriate Goals

The Malcom Baldridge Award[4] is an award that was established by the US Congress in 1987 to raise awareness of quality management and recognize US companies that implemented successful quality management systems. While well over 100 companies put the time and effort into attaining the award, many others determined not to pursue the award due to resource commitments, budgeting, and risk tolerance considerations. Similarly, improving maturity level goals can take a great deal of effort which the organization must be commit to. Operational leadership would prefer an Integrated (Level 5) maturity rating across all regions. Evaluate whether the organization is willing to dedicate the financial and resource commitments required in order to be fully integrated.

Here is one way to structure a clearly defined path and communicate what "good, better, and best" looks like and how you will get there. Consider completing an annual maturity model survey toward the end of the 3rd quarter. This allows you to summarize the results and create an action plan with regional support for improvements throughout the upcoming year. Tie the aligned action plan to your long-term project planning and resilience deployment process.

Set an attainable target for the upcoming year

Let us set a three-year plan for getting all the Professional Practices to a minimum Compliant level of 3.0. Since we have a total of ten practices, we will pick three of them to reach a minimum maturity level of 3.0 while we steadily improve upon the remaining seven as seen in Table 7.13.

Table 7.13 Annual maturity targets

Maturity of Excellence (MOE) 3-Year Continuous Improvement		
Annual Survey Cycle	Regionally Aligned Continuous Improvement Strategy	MOE Global Level
Base Year	* MOE survey completed by all regional facilities. * Results analyzed by region and globally. * Alignment on improvements through resilient deployment.	2.70
Year 1	* 3.0 for the most critical three Professional Practices. * Improvement on all remaining Professional Practices. * Monthly review of objectives tied to goals. * Quantitative and qualitative scorecard reporting.	2.83
Year 2	* 3.0 for the next three most critical Professional Practices. * +10% progress on Year 1 Professional Practices. * Monthly review of annual objectives. * Quantitative and qualitative scorecard reporting.	3.03

(Continued)

Table 7.13 (Continued)

Maturity of Excellence (MOE) 3-Year Continuous Improvement

Annual Survey Cycle	Regionally Aligned Continuous Improvement Strategy	MOE Global Level

Year 3
 	
Annual
  Resilient
  Deployment
	* 3.0 for the remaining four Professional Practices.
	* +10% progress on Year 2 Professional Practices.
	* Monthly review of annual objectives.
	* Quantitative and qualitative scorecard reporting.
	* Assess progress per three-year project plan.
	* Address obstacles encountered.
	* Communicate regional best practices across all operations.
	* MOE survey updated annually.
		3.30

Key Takeaways:

1. Scorecard reporting indicates progress toward maturity.
2. Maintain progress in a sustainable way.
3. Share regional pockets of expertise to share globally.
4. Look for ways to lead, follow, and guide teams toward greater maturity levels.

This should be attainable without a major strain on the participants' blocks of work, and it should not incur excessive costs. It is essential to have solid teams that are well engaged and trained along with planning that is tested and effective. We will focus on the following four goals in the upcoming year:

1. **Program Management Compliant to a minimum level of 3.0** – Identifying and supporting the right team members at the facility and regional level is a reasonable goal. Include primary and alternate team members in critical roles. Conduct monthly alignment meetings at local and leadership levels. Share results of the monthly scorecard tracking qualitative and quantitative scores. The blocks of work should be verified monthly with all team members. Ensure any new team members are working to complete their annual objectives.
2. **Awareness and Training Programs Compliant to a minimum level of 3.0** – Provide annual team training early in the year and include presentations, leadership messages, and videos. Include external stakeholders in the process. Respond to any issues raised in the maturity survey. Develop a method where training does not rely on a single individual to

be successful. Training should be conducted at global, regional, and facility levels for current and new team members throughout the year.

3. **Business Continuity Plan, Exercise, Assessment and Maintenance Compliant to a minimum level of 3.0** – Each facility should complete semi-annual tests of their plans with their leadership, external groups, and regional team members. Lessons learned from exercises should be tracked for completion and the results should be reported to operational leadership. Documentation on plan testing should be maintained in the business continuity software along with all continuous improvement suggestions.

4. **Maintain or improve upon remaining seven Professional Practices** – Keep momentum moving forward on every one of the practices. Share best practices across all regions during monthly and quarterly team meetings. Look for pockets of expertise and have them participate as keynote speakers whenever possible.

In our maturity model example above, the regional improvements would increase the global maturity level from 2.70 to 2.86 in the following year.

Look for continued improvement the following year

Align with the regions on selecting another three of the Professional Practices to be at a minimum Compliant level of 3.0. In addition, agree on improving the initial three from a minimum 3.0 by ten percent. Stretch your goals in several ways to keep making progress in operational resilience.

Keep momentum going into the third year

Identify activities that will support the remaining four of the ten Professional Practices to a minimum Compliant level of 3.0. In addition, agree on how you will improve the previous six by an additional 10 percent. The maturity level across all operations will be approaching a Proactive level in the third year.

Reassess your progress every year

Every year provides the opportunity to reassess the entire maturity model survey and project planning process. Changes in the organization provide opportunities to improve upon your objectives during the resilient deployment cycle. Make sure you are closely aligned with regional leadership to have the required management support, funding, and time commitments to keep charging ahead.

How to Lead, Follow and Guide the Way with Your Maturity Model

Develop and maintain a maturity model to track progress across the organization. Tie the process to your project planning and resilient deployment schedule. Engage all teams who participate in incidents, crises, and business continuity events to accurately assess elements that support each level of maturity.

o **Select maturity components.** Use a consistent measurement for evaluating maturity across your organization. Consider the DRI Professional Practices since they are a basis for individual and organizational resilience certifications. Ensure all teams are aware of each practice's objectives and operational resilience benefits. Maintain a current focus on all relevant standards and practices.

o **Define maturity levels.** Consider a maturity model with a five-point scale and universal method of collecting data. Clearly define all levels ranging from emerging to integrated. Define a progressive scale of maturity with clearly defined elements for each survey component. Train all regional facility teams to complete the survey. Suggest team involvement in every survey. Consolidate survey results by region and globally.

o **Determine "Good," "Better," and "Best".** Establish the initial survey results as your base year. Realize that it will require a great deal of time, resources, and funding to attain an integrated maturity level. Establish a baseline score across all regions and globally. Include actionable items to improve maturity levels as part of the objective setting process during the resilient deployment.

o **Set appropriate goals.** Set a three-year plan to steadily improve levels of maturity across the organization. Identify a Compliant goal for various Professional Practices that will help quickly promote maturity or improve upon big gaps in present maturity levels. Continue to focus on all maturity model elements in the next two years. Reevaluate progress through your annual resilient deployment cycle.

How to Lead

Construct a maturity model and survey that will improve upon the effectiveness of your business continuity and resilience process. Ensure it aligns with current business continuity, crisis, and risk management standards. Determine when to have operational teams complete the maturity survey in order to be the most effective. Create an effective way to communicate the maturity model and to conduct training to ensure it is well understood and will be accurately completed.

How to Follow

Review the maturity model levels, elements, and its business value with regional business continuity and operational leaders. Get their feedback and make any necessary modifications that still align with the organization's mission and goals. Align on the timing for implementing the maturity survey so that results can be integrated into the resilient deployment schedule.

How to Guide the Way

- Check on progress toward annual improvements in the maturity model during regularly scheduled meetings and reviews.
- Immediately address any concerns raised by regional teams that could stall their team's progress.
- Maintain an effective campaign toward attaining goals throughout the year.
- Prepare leadership messages and activities that support each of the elements to attain annual targets of improvement.
- Evaluate how your personal resilience experiences can support your team's efforts and communicate positive support for your teams.
- Celebrate successes and highlight behaviors as best practices throughout the organization.

Notes

1 https://drii.org/resources/professionalpractices/EN
2 https://drii.org/
3 https://www.merriam-webster.com/dictionary/maturity
4 https://www.nist.gov/baldrige

Chapter VIII

Maintaining Momentum

You have gotten to the point in your journey where short- and long-term planning for operational resilience is underway. You have gained leadership support. Teams are identified and well engaged, and all objectives are being met. Your teams are overcoming obstacles, and continuous improvement is part of the team's DNA. A maturity model is accurately in use to track internal progress. Your scorecard accurately reflects progress in attaining quantitative and qualitative objectives. The top operational risks are being planned for and are in focus by all personnel. The most critical business services and operations are identified, mapped, and effectively supported. Gaps are identified upon conclusion of events and crises and lessons learned are shared across all business units. You are at the point where there is excellence in operational resilience. You are leading, following, and guiding the way.

What's the next step? Continue to look for ways to be more supportive with the tools you use. Refine how you can be more effective in providing training, increasing awareness, and getting constructive feedback from your teams. Maintain a strong global alignment across all regions. Monitor evolving standards and external regulations that can be included in your steadily maturing and well-supported process. Increase your engagement with critical suppliers, customers, associates, their families, and the community.

In this chapter, we will provide suggestions on how the following concepts help to maintain momentum in creating or improving upon your operational resilience program.

- Internal Audit Surveys
- External Audits
- Business Continuity Action Lists
- Annual Risk-Based Activity (Hurricanes)
- Playbooks (ID)

DOI: 10.4324/9781003438700-8

- Environmental, Social, and Governance
- Artificial Intelligence (AI)
- Global Preparedness Month
- Benchmarking and Certification

Internal Audit Surveys

Internal audit is a highly respected business function that is skilled at examining and analyzing policies and procedures and providing results to the board and executive management. The audit team's role includes completing a thorough assessment of risks that could threaten the organization's mission, goals, objectives, and critical business components. Consider having an internal audit partner with you when conducting an independent analysis of your operational resilience program. Auditors can contribute a great deal by evaluating progress on your project plan and the accuracy of your maturity model levels. Regular internal audits provide assurance that competing priorities do not detract from commitments to operational resilience. Their objective analysis verifies your operations are ready to protect the organization from harm when crises occur. Additional value is gained from their ability to identify control gaps, ensure regulatory compliance, identify actions to improve maturity, and ensure business process owners are accountable for their planning, executing, and testing. You should follow the continuous improvement Plan, Do Check, Act model when engaging with internal audit in conducting an effective objective analysis of your operational resilience program.

Plan

The first quarter of each year is a good time to meet with your corporate general auditor's team and plan out an annual audit process. Internal auditors are skilled at executing an audit plan and adept at reading people. Provide the auditors with an audit survey checklist that includes individual audit objectives. Also include the inquiries that should be asked. Add the expectations that should be met to avoid audit findings for each objective. Finally, include any observations that may be relevant. All of this is combined in Table 8.1.

Once the audit survey checklist is prepared, conduct a meeting with all the auditors to review your expectations to complete the checklist. Set a schedule for facility audits. Notify the facility business continuity contacts and operational management so they are fully prepared for the audit. Internal auditors, the facility leadership, and BC contacts should understand the purpose of the audit in reinforcing awareness of BC as an important business process.

Table 8.1 Audit checklist

Internal Audit Survey Information
Date of interview:
Locations:
Interviewee/position:
Additional information:

#	Audit Objective	Inquiry	Expectations	Observations
1	Business continuity plan is updated.	Ask facility leader and business continuity contact to provide an overview of the plan, its contents, and its location.	Provide electronic documentation with evidence of support and engagement.	
2	Business continuity plan is tested.	Ask how the plan is tested, how often, and who is involved.	Show how the test was performed, the results, and next steps.	
3	Strong alignment exists between region and facility.	Check the facility leader and business continuity contact are implementing regional directives.	Provide evidence of participation in regional meetings and AOP alignment.	
4	New associates are aware of the facility's business continuity process.	Are all new hires trained in basic incident response and escalation actions?	Review documents used to train newly hired associates and ensure they are current.	
5	Facility business continuity team members are well engaged.	Interview team members to validate their interest and engagement in the business continuity process.	Team members are aware of requirements and have business continuity as part of their performance review.	
6	Business continuity roles have an adequate succession plan.	Determine if critical BC roles have a documented succession plan.	Verify the list of primary and alternate critical business continuity roles is currently maintained.	

(Continued)

Table 8.1 (Continued)

#	Audit Objective	Inquiry	Expectations	Observations
7	Evidence of local ISO or regulatory awareness exists.	Check ISO compliance and awareness of local regulations is evident.	Review documentation that will be shared with the ISO auditor and any other regulator.	
8	Business continuity software tool is current and updated.	Risk assessments, BIA, business continuity plans, and other documents are maintained in the planning software.	Review the latest facility risk assessment, BIA, and business continuity plan documents.	
9	External stakeholders are included in business continuity planning.	Are the external teams providing support included in business continuity plan related documents?	Review business continuity plans for inclusion of local contacts such as emergency services, health department, police, fire, etc.	
10	Formal training is in place for incidents, crises, business continuity events.	Are all personnel trained annually or more frequently to help support the team?	Validate annual training for present and new team members.	

Additional Notes:

Do

Add the business continuity audit review to the regularly scheduled financial audit that is planned each year. This avoids the need for additional budgeting or major time commitments. An audit announcement letter is sent to all parties involved in the upcoming audit and those who will be reviewing the audit results. The auditor makes observations, takes notes, reviews documents, and interviews associates during the visit. They analyze the risks and controls of the facility being audited and reviews compliance with all policies, laws, and regulations. They also verify the information provided is accurate and make recommendations on process improvements.

In addition to discussing the internal audit survey items above, the auditor will likely ask if the facility management or BC contact would like to share anything else regarding the current BC process. Some possible questions could include:

- Are they comfortable with how information is communicated between the facility, region, and global teams?
- Are there any specific risks that should be considered that are not already in planning stages?
- Are there any specific changes to the current BC process they would like to see?

See Table 8.2 for what auditors might include as findings for the four regional teams' part of our global manufacturing operations.

Check

Once the audit report is issued, the regional business continuity leader should work with each facility receiving an audit finding. They should close the loop on every finding, then provide a written response to the internal audit. Celebrate the success of every facility that has received no

Table 8.2 Audit findings

Category	Description	Region A Facility	Region B Facility	Region C Facility	Region D Facility
1	BC plan is not updated				
2	BC plan is not tested				
3	Lack of regional and facility alignment				
4	Lack of new associate training				
5	Lack of team member engagement				
6	No documented succession planning				
7	ISO compliance is not documented				
8	BC software is not up to date				
9	External stakeholders are not in BC plans				
10	Annual incident, crisis, and BC plan training is not completed				

Table 8.3 Regional audit scores

Internal Audit Monthly Qualitative Scorecard Finding Results				
Region	Number of Audits Completed	Total of All Questions Asked	Total of All Findings	Monthly Audit % Score
A	10	100	15	85
B	9	90	15	83
C	8	80	15	81
D	7	70	15	79

Note: In our example, there were a total of 15 findings in each region with the monthly scores being the % of audit objectives successfully completed.

audit findings. Remember to include the results of the audit in your monthly scorecard. See Table 8.3 for an example of calculating the audit scores. Let's consider our global manufacturer with four regions. We will assume there were a total of 15 audit findings in each of the regions. The number of facilities audited in the month varied as did the total number of audit questions asked. The resultant regional scores are calculated as the percent of audit objectives positively completed. In other words, the goal of the audit is to have no audit findings.

Act

Another benefit of the internal audit regional summary is that it shows the progress made on annual regional objectives. The results show gaps where greater focus may need to be placed in regional operational resilience planning. By following your resilient deployment schedule, you have a monthly opportunity to continue to take the steps needed to make regional improvements toward AOP objectives. Use the results of the internal audit reports to identify where additional resources or funding can help promote continuous improvement. Identify any best practices or comments from the internal audit you can share across all regions. Remember to celebrate successes and acknowledge the locations that have done outstanding work and are exceeding expectations. This is an excellent way to lead, follow, and guide the way.

External Audits

Global manufacturers and many other types of organizations receive resilience-based surveys from their customers. The surveys are sent to validate the effectiveness of business continuity Professional Practices. All organizations that are part of a customer's end-to-end supply chain can expect to receive surveys and to be audited. The surveys and audits have objectives

Table 8.4 Audit or survey crosswalk

External Audit or Survey Crosswalk
Date of survey or audit:
Locations:

#	Maturity Model and Professional Practice	Survey or Audit Requirement	Evidence or Documented Requirement	Observations
1	Program Management			
2	Risk Assessment			
3	BIA			
4	Business Continuity Strategies			
5	Incident Preparedness and Response			
6	Plan Development and Implementation			
7	Awareness and Training Programs			
8	Business Continuity Plan Exercise, Assessment and Maintenance			
9	Crisis Communications			
10	Coordination with External Agencies			

Additional Notes:

like our internal audit survey. The goal of every activity related to operational resilience is to be highly reliable and low maintenance. Our maturity model provides a regional status update on progress with the business continuity Professional Practices. Consider using Table 8.4 as a crosswalk document to compare external survey and audit requests to your maturity model. A crosswalk analysis is a way of comparing your process to others. It can include any of the components you want to benchmark in your program, including the metrics, key performance indicators, and maturity model components that have provided you success. A crosswalk document includes the requirement you have defined, along with the evidence or document reference you are comparing. It is an effective way to show what you are analyzing, how the components compare, and where gaps exist.

Business Continuity Action Lists

Throughout my journey in leading, following, and guiding teams toward operational resilience, I've seen risks, incidents and crises repeat themselves. As you manage incidents, crises, and business continuity events, you become aware of lessons learned and actions that can make your efforts in managing them next time more effective. Construct an action list of activities that you can share with your teams in advance of certain types of reoccurring risks. See Table 8.5 for an example of a Natural Incident Action List. Use it as a starting point and customize it to fit your organization.

Table 8.5 Natural incident action list

Natural Incident Action List (Hurricane, Typhoon, Tornado, Flood) Date of Activities Underway: Location:			
Issue/Action Item	*Assigned To*	*Date Due*	*Comments/ Status*

A. Planning Prior to the Incident
1. Incident Notification and Management
   • Be familiar with regional incident reporting and management programs.
   • Develop and regularly test incident management plans.
   • Be familiar with local warning signals and evacuation programs.
   • Prepare teams for local "storm duty" roles.
   • Designate staging areas for incident command.
   • Review offsite and work remote strategies.
2. Communications
   • Prepare a mass notification process.
   • Designate and train media spokespersons.
   • Prepare an external statement approval process.
   • Update media contact lists.
3. Associate Care
   • Provide evacuation and shelter in place training.
   • Implement a safety-first culture.
   • Provide a local first aid process.
   • Pre-establish an associate pay process.
   • Plan for assisting families of associates who remain onsite.
   • Develop a way to track traveling associates.
   • Determine critical roles and identify alternates.
4. Facility Operations
   • Document a utility isolation process.
   • Secure external objects.
   • Conduct inventory of critical equipment.
   • Prepare a centralized maintenance team.
   • Ensure perimeter security and access.			

(Continued)

Table 8.5 (Continued)

Issue/Action Item	Assigned To	Date Due	Comments/ Status

5. Business Continuity
  • Review planning with local and regional teams.
  • Coordinate emergency authorizations and approvals.
  • Review vendor contracts and alternate providers.
  • Prepare alternate sourcing strategies.
  • Review a quality approval and substitution process for production materials.
  • Store reserve fuel and other materials onsite.
  • Prepare for out-of-process cost tracking.			

6. Risk Management
  • Maintain current restoration and recovery contracts.
  • Align with property insurers on how to manage storm impact activities.
  • Develop pre-approvals for recovery activities.			

7. Additional Tactical Teams
  • Maintain updated business continuity plans.
  • Have primary and alternate team members prepared to engage as needed.			

B. Action During the Incident
1. Incident Management
  • Implement offsite emergency operations.
  • Implement the regional incident response, crisis management, or business continuity process as needed.			

2. Communications
  • Implement the mass notification process.
  • Maintain contact with onsite associates.
  • Prepare and obtain approvals for internal and external messaging.			

3. Associate Care
  • Implement activities to keep associates safe.
  • Provide required first aid and associate care.
  • Implement payroll plan.
  • Provide local counseling as needed.
  • Provide daily safety messages.
  • Monitor associates' abilities to work while managing family related issues.			

(Continued)

Table 8.5 (Continued)

Issue/Action Item	Assigned To	Date Due	Comments/ Status
4. Facility Operations • Ensure incident response activities are aligned with regulatory guidelines. • Monitor effectiveness of programs set in place prior to the incident. • Provide real-time reports on evolving facility issues.			
5. Information Technology • Activate local and regional service continuity plans where appropriate. • Monitor status of local equipment, applications, and tools needed to maintain effective communications. • Conduct damage assessments and make recommendations on repairs needed.			
6. Business Continuity • Manage the regional and global response and recovery process. • Be the liaison with the regional crisis management leader. • Provide a single update on all activities to have aligned support. • Determine workstreams and identify workstream leaders to ensure a well synched response and recovery is underway. • Schedule and manage meetings to provide support per approved policies and programs.			
7. Risk Management • Coordinate insurer-related activities including site adjustor work. • Work with financial teams on an approved cost tracking process.			
8. Additional Tactical Functions • Participate in response and recovery activities. • Provide expertise on minimizing cost and down time impact. • Bring additional team members into the workstream discussions to assist where needed.			
C. Action Taken After the Incident			
1. Incident Management • Conduct ongoing meetings with appropriate workstreams to maintain continuity of supply. • Implement local relationships for external assistance and regulatory approvals.			

(Continued)

Table 8.5 (Continued)

Issue/Action Item	Assigned To	Date Due	Comments/ Status
2. Communications • Continue to monitor media reports on local activities. • Advise on all internal and external messaging.			
3. Associate Care • Implement job safety analyses prior to equipment start up. • Provide safety messaging process. • Monitor physical and mental health of all local associates and those providing external support. • Provide financial support aligned with regional policy.			
4. Facility Operations • Coordinate all onsite regulatory activities. • Inspect all facilities prior to reoccupation. • Confer with quality teams on approvals to use materials and finished goods. • Complete hazard assessments before using equipment. • Ensure all utilities can be safely used.			
5. Information Technology • Ensure all onsite equipment is in good repair. • Coordinate local and regional service continuity activities. • Monitor equipment and application availability.			
6. Business Continuity • Align with operational leadership on when the business continuity and crisis management meetings can conclude. • Develop a post-incident survey to identify any gaps in planning. • Manage implementation of process improvements throughout the organization.			
7. Risk Management • Follow status of activities underway with adjustor and insurer to ensure seamless coordination until the claim is resolved. • Evaluate out-of-process cost tracking document.			
8. Additional Tactical Functions • Continue to support the local and regional teams until all issues are resolved.			
Additional Notes:			

Similar Action Lists for the following risks that can turn into common incidents for most organizations can also be of value:

- Active Assailant Action List
- Collective Bargaining Agreement (CBA) Action List
- Earthquake Action List
- Employee Assistant Program Action List
- Information Technology Action List
- Fire Protection Action List
- Flooding Incident Action List
- Political Escalation Action List
- Power Outage Action List
- Security Action List
- Supply Chain Action List

Engage the appropriate tactical functions in creating every Action List. Update them annually or whenever you have new and beneficial lessons learned from actual incidents. Share them with all team members and all regions.

Annual Risk-Based Activity (Hurricanes)

Numerous human, natural, and technological risks can have a major impact on your operations. You should consider developing an annual process to prepare your teams to effectively respond to them. Let's use preparing for a hurricane as an example, as they are a good example of a risk that can evolve into one of the most expensive incidents your organization will ever face.

The Federal Emergency Management Agency (FEMA) is a US governmental agency that supports our citizens and first responders to ensure that, as a nation, we work together to build, sustain, and improve our capability to prepare for, protect against, respond to, recover from, and mitigate all hazards.

The FEMA Hurricane planning site[1] is an excellent resource that provides hurricane related data, resources, and advice that helps maintain operational resilience. Hurricanes and typhoons are strong cyclones that occur in the Atlantic and Pacific oceans. Hurricanes follow the Saffir-Simpson Wind Scale with defined categories from 1 to 5 based on the hurricane's maximum and sustained winds. Various organizations and agencies provide annual predictions of the number of named hurricanes and their level of storm impact. Hurricanes rated a Category 3 and higher are known as major hurricanes that can cause catastrophic wind damage, storm surge, and loss of life. According to the National Hurricane Center[2], September

10 is the peak date for hurricanes. Forty percent of all tropical cyclones occur in September. Since 1842, 37 Category 5 hurricanes have been recorded, with severe wind levels of over 157 miles per hour. Twenty-five of those Category 5 hurricanes occurred in the month of September! For that reason, whatever the annual forecast, September is the month to be ready for hurricanes of greatest impact.

Goodyear associates and business operations are well prepared for hurricanes through an annual hurricane planning activity. Although the annual hurricane season occurs from June 1 through November 30, in recent years, winter storms which can match some of the major hurricanes in wind and storm surge impact have occurred. A well-developed and activated planning process for hurricanes can play a major role in your operational resilience process. Let's review how to get your teams prepared for hurricanes and gain benefits for other large-scale risks and incidents.

Organizing Your Annual Event

During the month of April of every year, I work with our regional and global teams on Goodyear's annual hurricane planning report out. We call it a report out since a meeting is set just prior to the hurricane season with operational leadership. It's an annual event where we have over a dozen tactical teams assess the current year's hurricane team response. In addition, each team shares insight on changes in their planning from the previous year and request any support they need from the other participants. It gets the entire team and region focused on planning for the current year so they can overcome any obstacles for executing strategies most effectively.

Preparing Your Teams

A global manufacturer may have over a dozen tactical teams participating in the annual hurricane planning process. To respect everyone's blocks of work, we schedule the meeting for an hour. A PowerPoint template deck is provided for each team to update in advance of the meeting. We ask each team to provide a three-minute overview of the following:

1. Main activities
2. Activation plan
3. Changes from the previous year
4. Any assistance needed from other teams or operational leadership

During the report out, the business continuity team captures all action items and provides the final PowerPoint deck to all participants. The organization's hurricane plan is ready and operational resilience is in focus.

Executing Your Hurricane Response

Many hurricanes provide advance warning, giving you enough time to initiate your plans. The National Hurricane Center provides warning up to seven days in advance for many hurricanes. The accuracy of hurricane landfall increases as the days to impact decreases. A five-day-to-landfall warning can quite accurately predict the general area at greatest risk. Mini hurricanes or microbursts can also occur. These hurricanes appear with little notice and can reach wind speeds of 100 miles per hour or greater. Over half of the hurricanes I've led, followed, and guided teams through caused spinoff tornadoes. Although your operations may not be anywhere near the point of hurricane landfall, the tornadoes can cause fatalities and major impacts to your facilities and business operations. According to the NOAA[3], of all the recorded weather disasters in US history, hurricanes have caused the most deaths and destruction.

For those reasons, natural incidents remain a top operational risk for most organizations. The work you put into preparing for them has multiple benefits. Planning for hurricanes allows you to follow and improve upon all the Professional Practices and maturity model components. The pre-planning, execution, and implementation of lessons learned are examples of a continuous improvement activity promoting operational resilience.

Playbooks (ID)

We've shown how business continuity playbooks are of value to your teams. The document includes more of the strategies, tactics, and methods teams can follow to maintain operational resilience. Let's recap parallel activities between success in sports and success in operational resilience.

A sports playbook defines what should be done to win a game. It includes actionable plays, roles, and responsibilities aligned with the team's strategies. A sports team succeeds when the coaches, players, and support personnel all execute plays as designed. The playbooks take all personnel into account and define their journey. You can consider it a part of their roadmap. A successful team effectively documents and communicates their goals. The goals are measurable, and teammates are held accountable for reaching them. Playbooks are powerful when they are visual and organized, and they communicate a message well. When teams use them effectively, the results include success in building new capabilities and improved performance.

There are similar benefits to every business in having well-developed playbooks for specific risks and incidents. The playbook helps the team visualize goals, focus on continuous improvement, and provide clarity on what success means. In our continuous improvement focus, the playbook is part of the planning component. Include data from benchmarking with other organizations when developing your playbook. Roles, responsibilities, and the execution of strategies are all critical components of your playbook. It should remain a living document since we know, just like risks continue to evolve, so do the strategies required to manage them and remain operationally resilient.

Let's use the risk of infectious disease as an example of how Goodyear's health services and business continuity teams worked closely with other tactical functions to develop an infectious disease playbook that continues to be used as a reliable reference document. Infectious disease is a term defined by **The Centers for Disease Control and Prevention (CDC)**[4] as illness caused by germs (such as bacteria, viruses, and fungi) that enters the body, multiplies, and causes an infection.

Goodyear's Medical Director brought his vision of building a culture of health around four components—health benefits, environmental health and safety, wellness, and emergency preparedness. He was quite pleased to see that our business continuity process included our associates as the focus when planning for incidents and crises. Supporting our associates through effective emergency management reduces risk of harm and helps them to stay resilient.

Our close partnership over the years included a common goal of making our associates our most valued asset and identifying actions needed to have a playbook to reference during the most far-reaching incident we ever faced, Covid -19. Let's use this as an example to outline the content needed for a risk or incident-based playbook to ensure you maintain momentum during the next far-reaching event. Continue to build, communicate, and use playbooks for additional risks and incidents that help execute plays more effectively and help to promote operational resilience.

ID Playbook:

Leadership Message

Engage a senior executive to deliver a message to all associates in your organization. Include an overview of what the playbook contains and who the intended audience is. Explain how it is part of business continuity and health services (medical) planning that must be kept current as a living document. Indicate that although some modifications may be made, the playbook includes practical recommendations based on a variety of sources, including the Centers for Disease Control and Prevention, the

World Health Organization[5], governments, and your business continuity and health services teams.

User Guide

Make the document interactive with links so that information can be accessed quickly.

Initiating the Plan

Reference how the plan is a coordinated response to help manage any localized infectious disease outbreak. Include examples like Norovirus, Hepatitis, Salmonella, Cholera, E-Coli, and various "flu" outbreaks that can escalate to pandemic levels. Plan for a well-coordinated response by internal and external teams. Conduct an assessment to determine the right response based upon the present risk of breakout. Once the level of response is determined, manage a risk-based response with appropriate workstreams similar to your major incident response. If the risk levels increase or decrease, take appropriate actions based on guidance and recommendations from trusted sources like the CDC, WHO, and community health services.

Commissioning the Response Team

Reference your BCP's policy for reporting major incidents which affect your associates and business operations. Regional or global business continuity teams will review the incident's impact and communicate next steps in response. Have an infectious disease outbreak team convene to conduct an initial review and determine next steps. Maintain communication throughout the process. The team members can vary based on the extent of the outbreak and business need. Regional teams generally consist of a leader who aligns with the region's crisis management team and provides guidance to facility teams. Facility planning teams focus on the health and safety of their associates, contractors, and their families and maintain close contact with local health and medical care providers. Follow the overall business continuity team engagement process.

Protocols

Include details of each of the following protocols after they are developed and approved by the appropriate cross-functional team and leadership:

- Pausing or closing operations.
- Case reporting, investigation, and management.

- Remote work capabilities.
- Personal protective equipment.
- Cleaning, disinfection, and sanitization.
- Social and physical distancing.
- Facility engineering and environmental controls.
- Site access controls.
- Business travel.

Managing the Workplace

Reference when working remotely will be required or optional. Include the process to be followed when an infectious disease outbreak has concluded, and governmental agencies have approved returning to work. Evaluate when the facility is ready to reopen and if appropriate policies and procedures have been implemented.

Training and Communication

Maintain clear communication with all internal and external audiences, including your associates, customers, suppliers, shareholders, and authorities. Integrate the communications team into your business continuity process to provide advice on all messages delivered and tactics used. Include leadership messages and videos, social media, responses to customer and supplier inquiries, and training documents. Develop a return-to-work training plan for associates with information on how to safely return to the workplace, and clearly describe what steps have been taken to keep the workplace safe and healthy. It also can provide them with information on what to expect about the new workplace and can highlight any changes implemented due to the new protocols.

Governance and Continuous Improvement

Provide a list of governance activities (e.g., vaccinations, facility closures, implementing protocols, etc.) to manage the evolving changes expected during an infectious disease outbreak. These activities help give the leadership team evidence that response plans in place are working as they should. Conduct a gap analysis to promote continuous improvement. Develop a series of audits and inspections to validate the new protocols.

Additional Resources

Include all external references that will be followed globally as the baseline for the infectious disease playbook.

Environmental, Social, and Governance

Always be on the lookout for common operational resilience initiatives throughout your organization. For example, it is mutually beneficial for Environmental, Social, and Governance (ESG) and a well-established BCP to partner with each other. ESG supports the sustainability of people and the planet through a variety of initiatives, and business continuity has expertise in some of the voluntary ESG activities that are tied to investment decision making and securing capital.

ESG references risks that can be included in your resilience deployment process, including carbon emissions, climate-related risks, conflict minerals, human rights, and employment risks. Here is an example of a climate change survey where your business continuity team can help the sustainability team provide an accurate response that supports operational resilience.

What is a climate change related risk?

You can experience operational facility losses through hurricanes and other severe weather events. The losses can consist of deceased revenues due to reduced demand for finished goods, increased pricing for raw materials, and property repairs.

Describe the physical risk exposure

Describe your global manufacturing footprint consisting of four regions. Include how all the facilities can experience weather impacts even though they implement operational resilience programs. Describe the types of operational impacts within the past few years due to severe weather.

What is the potential financial risk impact?

Include actual and potential cost impact figures based on historical frequency and levels of severity. Reference what you factor into calculations, including anticipated business growth and inflation.

Describe your organization's response

Describe your business continuity process and response to severe weather events. Include the annual budget for the program. Provide an overview of how proactively identifying risks and critical processes speeds up response and recovery and minimizes cost impact. Integrating risk-based decision making helps identify and close potential gaps that could have long-term cost savings that in turn support your ESG goals.

Artificial Intelligence (AI)

Artificial Intelligence (AI) is defined by IBM[6] as a field, which combines computer science and robust datasets, to enable problem solving. It also encompasses sub-fields of machine learning and deep learning, which are frequently mentioned in conjunction with artificial intelligence. These disciplines are comprised of AI algorithms which seek to create expert systems which make predictions or classifications based on input data. AI is of business value when it assists people in solving real issues by exhibiting human-like intelligence and behavior through machine learning, analyzing data, and high-speed information gathering.

AI can support operational resilience by being more predictive of risks, more responsive to crises, and more resilient to disruptions. By using big data analytics and algorithms, more accurate forecasting can be made. Future events and crises can be predicted. AI can be used to evaluate business continuity plans and assign the optimum resources to respond most effectively. IT service continuity and disaster recovery planning can be improved by using AI algorithms to monitor IT systems and networks and predict faults before they occur. Backup systems and processes can be automated to avoid loss of data. Methods of continuously updating these and many more business continuity practices through big data analytics, automating processes, and machine learning are evolving. It is critical to involve your IT and legal teams to keep security, privacy, and ethics in focus as AI evolves. See how you can add AI concepts to your policies and procedures. Use AI concepts to lead, follow, and guide the way toward excellence in operational resilience.

Global Preparedness Month

During September of every year, FEMA promotes a campaign known as "National Preparedness Month" as an observance to raise awareness about the importance of preparing for disasters and emergencies that could happen at any time. Through the **Ready.gov website**[7], FEMA provides a toolkit of suggested messages, posters, and other materials to help every organization inform their associates of the benefits of being prepared. FEMA publishes their annual theme about a month before September's campaign. Consider using their theme or one you believe is of value based on recent operational crises you've experienced. The example below is based upon a theme FEMA suggested a few years ago following the theme: "Disasters Happen. Prepare Now. Learn How."

Maintain momentum toward operational resilience by engaging all your global associates in a similar campaign. Let's use our global manufacturer with four regions as an example. Coordinate with your regional communication and business continuity teams on the messages to be delivered, the method of delivering them, and timing for sharing them with all associates.

Start by developing a leadership message that references the campaign. Include an explanation of Global Preparedness Month and why it's of interest to all your regional associates in your global operations. Share what the weekly messages throughout the month will be. Encourage all recipients to share it with their family and friends. State it will be available through emails and various other social media platforms. Encourage sharing it during team meetings, shift changes, and team daily management meetings.

Here is an example of four weekly messages tied to the monthly campaign:

Week 1: Preparing Yourselves and Your Families

Make and practice a family game plan for emergencies that occur at home. Learn lifesaving skills that can benefit you and your family. Know and review plans for schools and the community. Prepare financially for potential impacts of an emergency.

Week 2: Travel Considerations

Leverage your websites to be aware of travel-related issues and how to avoid or minimize their impacts. Know who to contact for assistance in case of emergencies when traveling internationally. Review driver and passenger safety and security advice.

Week 3: Business Continuity at Work

Provide tips for testing plans at both home and work. Know how business continuity teams tie their planning together in an effective way to ensure they are prepared for risks.

Week 4: Coordination with External Agencies

Learn which local organizations are prepared to help you advance your initiatives and be ready to work with them. Discuss how you can provide feedback to improve community-based emergency planning.

Also encourage all regions and their facilities to have an event where they bring in external authorities (e.g., police, fire, health departments, Red Cross, etc.) on a designated day of the month and devote a couple of hours to allowing them to review presentations, receive materials, and ask questions that relate to the monthly campaign.

By providing focus on a common theme that benefits your associates, you've taken a major step in educating and training your organization's most valuable asset—its associates.

Benchmarking and Certification

Benchmarking helps promote continuous improvement

Throughout your operational resilience journey, you're constantly leading, following, and guiding the way. You benchmark your process to continuously improve the tools you use, develop training for your teams, and increase the value of your program across the organization. It's as simple as defining where you are today, determining where you want to be in the future, and coming up with a plan to get there. Measuring internal progress as well as knowing how your process ranks with world-class organizations can help you keep goals current and attain them faster. Our global manufacturer example can be benchmarked to certain standards in its industry. Compare yourself to not only your competitors, but also to other sectors and industries that are clearly resilient. Our manufacturer can benefit by comparing its project plan and maturity model to organizations in hospitality, education, legal, construction, finance, retail, insurance, and health care sectors for example. The goal of benchmarking is continuous improvement. You will either make changes to promote process improvement or validate you are on the right track.

An example of how different sectors can work together can be demonstrated by the opportunity I had to work closely with the Association of Independent Colleges and Universities of Ohio (AICUO)[8] after being on a task force for the State of Ohio on pandemic planning. The task force had a cross-functional team representing all sectors that developed a plan in the event a pandemic were to spread and affect residents and businesses in Ohio. AICUO saw a parallel between my incident planning and what was needed at the colleges they represent. The relationship we established led to me working with AICUO's independent colleges on tabletop exercises, incident management, and other resilience-based activities. We realized that the ability to recover, adjust to change, and bounce back effectively from an incident or crisis is a common goal. We use similar tools and strategies regardless of our business function. Our associates, students, customers, and business partners expect us to be at our best regardless of the risks and incidents we face.

Get your teams involved in the process by leading, following, and guiding the way. Conduct an annual assessment of your process through benchmarking. Start by defining what will be benchmarked. The next step includes reviewing the status of the activities you're benchmarking with associates, competitors, customers, suppliers, and others that appear to be the best at what they do. Once you gather relevant data, analyze it and determine where you may need to make modifications to improve your process. Your action plan should include any necessary changes to your project plan and the multi-year objectives and goals that are part of them. Make them part of your resilient deployment process to give them visibility and inclusion into your formal goal setting process.

Certification shows industry related knowledge and commitment

Individual certification is a method of being recognized and receiving credentials for a significant accomplishment. The certification includes validation through a testing process that is attained with verification of a required level of experience and education. There are many advantages to the individual and the organization for having certified professionals in your field of expertise, including proof of industry knowledge, heightened credibility, work ethic, and peer recognition. It also provides an individual the ability to apply for many jobs requiring a minimum certification level. The work put into attaining certifications correlate to having the skills necessary to develop and manage project plans, formulate strategies and complete objectives. It shows commitment to their field of study and to the industry. Maintaining certifications requires attending seminars, conferences, or workshops or completing activities that show a level of expertise in their field. The activities involve staying up to date on evolving industry trends. Some organizations share proprietary materials that can only be accessed by those with certain certifications.

Organizational certification is a validation that a specific part of the organization (or entire organization) has fulfilled the requirements of the standards established by the credentialing entity to attain the certification. An example is International Organization for Standardization (ISO) 9001 certification[9] which establishes product conformance to standardized requirements. The product also refers to services, materials, hardware, and software. Organizational certifications establish credibility and trust with many global manufacturers that require their suppliers to meet annual certification requirements through independent testing agencies.

Determine the certification that's right for you

There are various levels of active professional certifications for many of the tactical functions supporting operational resilience we discussed in this book.

The list below is not all encompassing. Each of the professions have their own peer networks and their own process for recognizing excellence in their professional fields.

- DRI International[10]: Business continuity, crisis management, incident management, operational resilience.
- BCI[11]: Similar to DRI above.
- RIMS[12]: Risk management, insurance.
- ASIS[13]: Security.
- IAEM[14]: Emergency management.
- ISC[15]: Information security.
- Supply Chain[16]: Supply chain, logistics, transportation.

Our maturity model is based on the Professional Practices[17] which are available on the DRI International site. DRI certification is a two-part process including verification of knowledge and confirmation of experience. They offer over a dozen types of certifications for public and private sector individuals in business continuity practice, business continuity audit, cyber resilience, healthcare continuity, public sector continuity, and risk management.

How to Lead, Follow and Guide the Way to Maintain Momentum in Operational Resilience

Look for ways to be better engaged and supportive of the overall operational resilience process. Maintain a strong alignment between every region, their teams, and your associates. Monitor changes to present regulations that affect your operations and other business sectors. Remain focused on continuous improvement in everything you do.

- o **Internal Audit Surveys.** Partner closely with your internal audit teams to validate results of scorecards and maturity surveys. Provide internal audit with training and audit tools so they can provide greater assurance that you have effective coverage to protect the organization from harm through operational resilience programs. Include internal audit results and findings as objectives in your monthly scorecard. Verify your project plan is on track.
- o **External Audit Surveys.** Use the work done in your maturity model as a basis to respond to external audits and surveys. Construct a crosswalk document to compare your maturity model and Professional Practices with external audits and surveys. Include the evidence or documents required in the comparison of each item. You will see this is a highly reliable and low maintenance comparative tool.

o **Business Continuity Action Lists.** Develop easy to use checklists that include how to prepare for, respond to, and recover from common risks and incidents. Consider having action lists for all of the top operational risks in your organization. Update the action lists annually or whenever significant improvements are observed during large scale events and crises. Share them with all business regions and teams so the entire organization benefits from the work done by any of your teams.

o **Annual Risk Based Activity.** Select a risk that has far-reaching effects on your associates and business operations. Schedule an annual event where all teams supporting the planning, response, and recovery will present their overview of activities in preparing for the event, any changes from the previous year, and any help needed from the other teams. Capture any new activities into the appropriate action list as part of process improvement.

o **Playbooks.** Build playbooks to further expand your action lists for top operational risks. Use infectious disease as an example since it was global in scale, impacted the entire world including your organization, and will be of interest and value to all your teams. Each playbook should include visible leadership support and a user guide, along with guidance on how to initiate the plan, manage it through closure, identify gaps, and share lessons learned. Conduct an annual review of each playbook, or at a greater frequency if significant changes occur that should be included in the playbook.

o **Environmental, Social, and Governance (ESG).** Embrace evolving voluntary and regulatory programs like ESG in support of operational resilience. Harness the value of project planning in your journey with business continuity, risk management, crisis management, and other related programs. Voluntary programs often become regulatory, so establish your organization as a leader in the programs they see value in supporting.

o **Global Preparedness Month.** Develop an annual campaign to focus on your associates and explain how they are integral to the success of your resilience. Work with your communications team to develop weekly messages and share them with associates throughout the world. Let everyone know that the focus in all planning and recovery efforts are your associates and their families. Encourage them to share the weekly messages and be better prepared at home, at work, and while traveling. Encourage them to provide feedback for upcoming campaigns.

o **Benchmarking and Certification.** Continuous improvement includes verifying how your process compares with your competitors, customers, and those considered best in class. Benchmarking your project plan, objectives, and maturity model annually will either validate you are on track or demonstrate you need to make changes to be more effective.

Certifications for your team members and your organization add tremendous value by acknowledging competencies of your teams and organization. They are a way of validating standards of excellence that are recognized by all progressive organizations and your peers.

How to Lead

Look for ways to maintain momentum with all the work your teams have done to be operationally resilient. Develop an internal audit survey that includes the key components of your maturity model. Train the audit team in using the survey. Prepare a crosswalk document to compare your maturity model components with external audits and surveys. Plan an annual risk-based activity to prepare your teams to focus on a top operational risk each year. Evaluate how your project planning supports evolving voluntary and mandatory programs. Work with communications teams to create annual associate readiness. Structure internal and external benchmarking tools to improve your program. Analyze which certifications will benefit your team members and organization.

How to Follow

Present the internal audit surveys to the internal auditors, get their feedback, and update the documents they will use. Monitor which external surveys are received and allow your teams to complete them and provide feedback on their effectiveness. Make changes to your annual operational risk program based on feedback received from your teams. Allow the supporting teams to provide input on all playbooks and action lists. Update the documents with feedback from voluntary and regulatory compliance standards. Get feedback from all associates on the value of global preparedness month campaigns. Review your project planning and maturity model based on annual benchmarking. Support your teams in obtaining the most applicable certifications to benefit the organization.

How to Guide the Way

Consolidate responses from teams into a common crosswalk document. Manage the annual operational risk review and have all teams be on standby to engage when needed. Update all playbooks and action lists, making them available for all regions to use. Participate in all voluntary and evolving surveys and programs that tie to operational resilience. Provide awareness and training through an annual preparedness month campaign and keep associates engaged throughout the year. Compare your project plan and maturity survey with those considered to be best in class.

Create awareness of individual and organizational certifications for your operational leadership. Gain the benefit of every program, process, and initiative we presented in this book. Evaluate how your personal resilience experiences can support your team's efforts and communicate positive support for your teams. Celebrate successes and highlight behaviors as best practices throughout the organization.

Notes

1 https://www.fema.gov/emergency-managers/risk-management/hurricanes#:~:text=The%20National%20Hurricane%20Program%20(NHP,territorial%20and%20federal%20government%20partners
2 https://www.nhc.noaa.gov/
3 https://www.noaa.gov/
4 https://www.cdc.gov/
5 https://www.who.int/
6 'What is Artificial Intelligence (AI)?', IBM, https://www.ibm.com/topics/artificial-intelligence#:~:text=At%20its%20simplest%20form%2C%20artificial,in%20conjunction%20with%20artificial%20intelligence
7 https://www.ready.gov/september#:~:text=National%20Preparedness%20Month%20is%20an,could%20happen%20at%20any%20time
8 https://www.aicuo.edu/
9 https://www.iso.org/iso-9001-quality-management.html
10 https://drii.org/
11 https://www.thebci.org/training-qualifications/cbci-online.html
12 https://www.rims.org/resources/strategic-enterprise-risk-center
13 https://www.asisonline.org/
14 https://www.iaem.org/certification/intro
15 https://www.isc2.org/Certifications/CISSP/Experience-Requirements
16 https://www.ismworld.org/certification-and-training/certification/cpsm/
17 https://drii.org/resources/professionalpractices/EN

Chapter IX

Conclusion

Call to Resilience

Resilient individuals and organizations have a few things in common, including being most effective when they face challenges. They maintain control when others may not, and behave in a way that makes others want to join them in their journey. When your organization is operationally resilient, all activities are integrated under a common structure. It is a long-term commitment by an organization to a well-developed and consistently implemented process. Core competency behaviors play a major role in resilience. Focus on situational awareness, agility, promoting collaboration, energizing teams, and delivering results. Leading, following, and guiding the way includes having the knowledge of what to do, gaining team feedback, and staying aligned on your forward plan.

Throughout the book, we referenced operational risks of concern to every organization. The resilience journey and roadmap include long-term project planning and tools to help promote a better understanding of how you will create, maintain, or improve upon resilience in your operations. Your initial steps in your journey include documenting your policy and charter and building a project plan. Frequent status updates on your annual objectives allow operational leadership to know if there are any issues where they can step in and assist. A blocks of work summary creates awareness of time commitments and can show the value of having personnel supporting common objectives. Integrate the continuous improvement mindset in every activity.

Individuals and companies make subconscious risk-based decisions. Formularize your risk-based decision making with other teams in your organization under a common process and turn risks into opportunities. Ensure you have a common definition of incidents, crises, and business continuity events. Track your operational incidents and crises accurately since they help you determine top operational risks. Include unexpected or novel risks in resilience planning since outbreaks of infectious disease, invasions of countries, and being held hostage through ransomware were considered novel risks and are now commonplace.

DOI: 10.4324/9781003438700-9

Analyze your entire organization and determine how to structure your teams to help promote operational resilience. Establish a method of governance and a global structure that cascades through all operations. Find your subject matter experts in critical roles and make them part of the team. Get leadership on board with the right reporting structure to show the commitment needed to be successful.

Establish an annual resilient deployment process with documented plans across all operations. Create a project plan that starts with a long-term plan that includes short-term and immediate priorities. Develop an annual operating plan with current year objectives that are part of your scorecard reporting process. Include quantitative and qualitative activities in monthly reporting. Conduct risk assessments, identify critical business processes, and build plans for recovery when needed. Conduct impact tolerance testing to validate maximum tolerable levels of disruption. Use scalable business continuity planning based on the criticality of business operations and the number of associates in each operation. Manage resilient deployment meetings by having a regular cadence of monthly, quarterly, and annual meetings.

Have a common objective with performance metrics for all associates in critical roles supporting operational resilience. Get senior leadership on board supporting the time commitment to operational resilience. Build out global and regional business continuity time commitments through your blocks of work. Expect your team members to actively represent their functions and workstreams whenever needed. Rely on your personal experience and motivators to help create a resilient mindset as you lead, follow, and guide the way.

Develop and use a maturity model to track progress from evolving to reactive, followed by compliant, proactive, and finally an integrated level. Select maturity components like the Professional Practices and define what it means to be "good, better, and best" in each practice. Set appropriate goals for improvement per your project plan. Gain alignment through resilient deployment and make adjustments that comply with the organization's risk appetite.

Keep momentum moving forward by partnering with your internal audit teams to validate project planning is understood, cascades through the organization and promotes progress. Respond to external surveys on resilience through an accurate and current crosswalk document. Conduct annual activities and awareness campaigns to keep your teams ready for the right risks. Look for evolving voluntary and regulatory programs that can benefit from your successes in operational resilience. Benchmark similar organizations and other business sectors every year and continuously improve upon your present programs. Get certified as individuals and as an organization to network, benchmark, stay current on industry trends, and increase your credibility.

Now that I've shared what's worked for me over many, many years, are you ready to lead, follow, and guide the way to attain excellence in operational resilience? I wish you the very best in doing so.

The only thing harder than being resilient is explaining why you aren't.
Michael W. Janko, author and resilient leader

Index

Pages in *italics* refer to figures and pages in **bold** refer to tables.

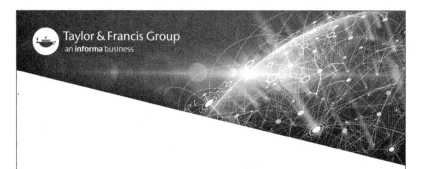

Printed in the United States
by Baker & Taylor Publisher Services